MW00424681

My Odyssey through History

My Odyssey through History

MEMOIRS OF WAR AND ACADEME

CHARLES P. ROLAND

Louisiana State University Press ✦ Baton Rouge

Copyright © 2004 by Louisiana State University Press
All rights reserved
Manufactured in the United States of America
First printing

05   07   09   11   13   12   10   08   06   04
2   4   5   3   1

DESIGNER: Barbara Neely Bourgoyne
TYPEFACE: Galliard
PRINTER AND BINDER: Thomson-Shore, Inc.

LIBRARY OF CONGRESS CATALOGING-IN-PUBLICATION DATA:

Roland, Charles Pierce, 1918–
  My odyssey through history : memoirs of war and academe / Charles P. Roland.
    p. cm.
  ISBN 0-8071-2853-8 (alk. paper)
  1. Roland, Charles Pierce, 1918– 2. Historians—United States—Biography.
3. Educators—United States—Biography. 4. World War, 1939–1945—Personal
narratives, American. 5. Soldiers—United States—Biography.   I. Title.
  E175.5.R75R65 2004
  973.7'092—dc21
                                                            2003013195

The paper in this book meets the guidelines for permanence
and durability of the Committee on Production Guidelines for
Book Longevity of the Council on Library Resources. ♾

Dedicated to the entire Roland clan,
my comrades of the 99th Infantry Division,
my classroom colleagues, my students,
and all my friends

Contents

Illustrations

With Gloria and Otis Singletary

With war comrade Samuel Lombardo

With Genevieve and Kent Masterson Brown

With war comrade Neil Brown

Foreword

Charles Pierce Roland is in many ways representative of his generation. He grew to manhood in the Great Depression, served in the armed forces in World War II, returned to school after the war, married, and won success in his professional career. Yet Roland brings to this memoir an unusual, perhaps unique, blend of scholarly qualifications, personal experiences, and longevity. Born in 1918 in Tennessee, he fought in Europe in World War II, taught history at three major universities (briefly at Louisiana State University and for eighteen years each at Tulane University and the University of Kentucky), held visiting professorships at the United States Military Academy and the United States Military History Institute and Army War College, wrote books and articles that won scholarly acclaim, and continues to lecture and write.

In these engaging recollections, Roland describes his early years in the small-town South of rural West Tennessee, collegiate education at Freed-Hardeman Junior College and at Vanderbilt University, where he first felt the satisfaction of academic achievement, and employment in the depression as an insurance salesman, high school teacher, and historical aide for the National Park Service in Washington, D.C., a broadening, nearly idyllic interlude brought to an end by World War II. After induction into the United States Army in early 1942 and military training in Georgia, Mississippi, Louisiana, and Texas, he served as a combat infantry officer in Belgium and Germany. No doubt this was the most challenging time of his life; certainly, it was the most dangerous. He received the Bronze Star for meritorious service and the Purple Heart medal for wounds received in action.

Captain Roland's division, the green 99th Infantry, landed in Europe in late 1944, several months after the Allied invasion of Normandy. It initially encountered sustained enemy action in the Ardennes region in Belgium in December 1944, when the German army launched the massive counteroffensive that turned into what later became known as the "Battle of the Bulge." The assault first struck the position occupied by Roland's regiment. Roland traces his division's desperate, fateful resistance to the surprise attack; subsequent retreat and stubborn six-weeks' defense of Elsenborn Ridge, a critical position that the historian Stephen Ambrose, alluding to the battle of Gettysburg, called "the Little Round Top of the Ardennes campaign"; crossing of the Rhine River under artillery fire at Remagen Bridge; and soldiering on in the invasion of Germany. His account is gripping: a story of suffering and death stemming from exposure to cold and the dangers and deprivations of prolonged life in the field; confusion and chaos of battle; friendships forged and comrades lost; fear and fatalistic courage under fire. Through it all, Roland focuses on his fellow citizen soldiers. "The marvel is that the draftee divisions were able to generate and maintain any esprit de corps at all," he observes with the seasoned insight of a participant and veteran military historian. "Formed originally by mixing men indiscriminately from throughout the nation, thus severing all personal, social, community, and regional bonds," their ranks replenished in combat by equally "depersonalizing" arrangements, "their only source of morale, other than the shared hazard and hardship, was the character and patriotism of the soldiers, rank and file. Fortunately, that proved to be sufficient."

Almost four years after he entered the army, Roland returned from Europe late in 1945 to civilian life in his Tennessee hometown. The war had changed his life forever. Exhilaration at being alive and at loose ends was soon followed by depression brought on by "the sudden descent from the powerful intoxication of war. . . . The only excitement left was to eat, drink, and be merry." When the pleasures of this recourse faded, Roland returned to Washington of golden memory, reclaimed his old job with the National Park Service, and enrolled as a graduate student in history at George Washington University. Again, satisfaction eluded him. Then, encouraged by offhand advice, he transferred to Louisiana State University in Baton Rouge to study history. Though he had known nothing of the history department at LSU before his arrival there, the move was serendipitous. He found an outstanding faculty and a cast of stimulating graduate students, some of whom became lifelong friends. He studied southern history, first under the direction of Bell I. Wiley, a highly regarded historian of southern blacks during the Civil War and of the common soldier of the Confederacy, and then, after Wiley's departure, under the eye of Francis Butler Simkins, a legendary eccentric whose fertile insights into the sources of the South's cultural and political distinctiveness had made him one of the most original and provocative historians of the region.

In this setting, Roland found an enduring sense of purpose: He wanted to teach history. Serendipity prevailed in other ways as well. Roland married "the most beautiful and most lovable" woman he had ever seen. A person of keen intelligence and exceptionally sound judgment, she became a source of unwavering support. Even his recall to active military duty in the Korean War, while he was completing his doctoral dissertation, turned to Roland's advantage. Thanks to his military experience and the good offices of Wiley, his former teacher, Roland spent his tour of duty in Washington as assistant to the chief historian of the United States Army, an assignment that advanced his career as a historian and afforded him valuable professional connections.

The final sections of the memoir trace Roland's career after his appointment in 1952 to the ambitious, rising history faculty at Tulane University. The Rolands loved life in New Orleans; he prospered at Tulane. Excellence in teaching and the favorable reception given his books and articles on the Civil War carried him up the academic ladder to the rank of professor. Things turned sour in the late 1960s, while Roland served as chairman of the Department of History. Embattled by turmoil on campus and conflict and upheaval in his department, he resigned from Tulane and accepted a distinguished professorial appointment at the University of Kentucky in Lexington. There he resumed doing the things he most enjoyed, teaching and writing, activities that he has continued with characteristic vigor, the teaching until the end of his visiting professorship at West Point in 1992, the writing until today.

I first met Professor Roland in 1959, when I entered graduate school at Tulane University. It was the beginning of a long and close association. Roland was a superb lecturer. His resonant voice, narrative skill, and use of telling quotations and striking vignettes made his lectures memorable. He had something to say, and he said it with the eloquence and clarity that sprang from knowledge of subject and much thought about it. Possessed of a philosophical cast of mind, belief in the cross-grained character of humanity, and sensitivity to history's unintended consequences, Roland shunned the occupational temptation to treat the past as a morality play. Instead, he emphasized the complexities of human motivation and action in a manner that conveyed humane values, inspired hope, and cautioned against cynicism or unrestrained optimism.

To the guidance of graduate students working on their doctoral dissertations, Roland brought similar attributes. He welcomed students who differed from him in outlook, and he did so not because it was easy or expedient, but because of genuine acceptance and lack of desire to replicate himself. Though soft-spoken and of courtly, if unadorned, manner, he was an incisive, tough-minded critic of his students' written work. If lessons taught were not always lessons learned, no one who wrote under his direction could fail to benefit from his criticism, unerring detection of the weak argument, insistence on clarity of expression, and commitment to objectivity and the need to tell the truth.

Roland took graduate students and their work seriously, but with agile wit and timely advice he discouraged them from taking themselves too seriously. In doing so, he taught memorable lessons that sometimes went beyond academic work. To those who repeatedly complained of uncertainty about where to incorporate in their dissertations a point that was especially hard to place, Roland often solemnly replied, "Save it for the last chapter." This frustrating advice usually worked. By the time the student arrived at the final chapter, the seemingly intractable problem had usually vanished, absorbed along the way by new perspectives, or set aside, the welcome casualty of attrition. Students who shrank from reaching potentially unfashionable conclusions apparently merited by their research were sometimes met with a biblical aphorism drawn from an evangelical heritage: "The wicked flee when no man pursueth, but the righteous are bold as a lion." To a doctoral candidate who defended his slow progress, earnestly explaining that the competing claims of conflicting evidence were forcing him to "struggle with his conscience," Roland shot back with an amiable smile, "My God! What a monstrous mismatch!"

The ability and hard work that brought Roland success as a teacher produced similar results in his books and articles. They consistently embody his approach to history: conscientious efforts, set in the particularity of the time and place and culture, to understand and explain what happened and why, without advocacy, censure, or self-aggrandizing moralism. His first book, *Louisiana Sugar Plantations during the American Civil War*, a pioneering work on Confederate agriculture, won the state library association's Louisiana Literary Award for "the best book published on Louisiana during 1957." Three years later his second book, *The Confederacy*, was published. Its vivid narrative and deft management of clashing interpretations of the Confederate experience made it one of the strongest volumes in the University of Chicago Press's acclaimed *Chicago History of American Civilization* series. Roland turned to biography in 1964 with *Albert Sidney Johnston: Soldier of Three Republics*, the book he regards as his best. The product of extensive research and a model of judicious assessments of the Confederate general, it was named in 1981 by *Civil War Times Illustrated* and in 1995 by *Civil War: The Magazine of the Civil War Society* as one of the best one hundred books on the Civil War.

In his next two volumes, Roland took up the history of the South. His revision (1972) of Francis Butler Simkins's badly dated textbook *A History of the South* again made it what many regarded as the best single-volume study of the region. Three years later he drew on his own research and the burgeoning body of literature on the recent South to produce a broad survey, *The Improbable Era: The South since World War II* (1975). Historians gave it a favorable reception. Harvard professor David Herbert Donald called it "the most comprehensive and the most objective account of the South during the past generation I have ever read." After Roland retired from the faculty, he returned to his first scholarly love, the Civil War, with *An American Iliad: The Story of the Civil War* (1991), the elegantly written, mature fruit of years of research and thought. Gary W. Gallagher, a leading scholar of the war, voiced an opinion echoed by other specialists in the field when he characterized it as the "best introduction to the nation's great trauma." In 1995, Roland entered the lively scholarly debate on the character and generalship of General Robert E. Lee with his *Reflections on Lee: A Historian's Assessment* (1995). It is, according to one expert on the Civil War, "a delightful volume, filled with insights and firmly grounded in decades of scholarship, teaching, and, yes, reflection by one of the nation's foremost authorities on the Civil War" and "a balanced assessment of Robert E. Lee's strengths and weaknesses as a man and soldier." Roland's last book, *Jefferson Davis's Greatest General: Albert Sidney Johnston,* published in 2000, is an abbreviated version of his biography of the Confederate general.

The caliber and range of Roland's publications—stretching from the emergence of the South as a distinctive section in the early Republic through the 1960s—established him as one of the most versatile and distinguished historians of the South. Reviewers and commentators have consistently labeled his publications "authoritative," "masterly," "incisive," and "learned"; praised their objectivity, balance, quality of synthesis, conciseness, and graceful exposition; and frequently identified him as one of the nation's foremost scholars in his fields. Publication as revised or reprinted editions of four of his eight major books confirms these judgments: *Louisiana Sugar Plantations during the Civil War* (1997), *Albert Sidney Johnston* (2001), *An American Iliad* (2002), and *Reflections on Lee* (2003).

A brief, thoughtful retrospective helps to account for this achievement. It identifies many of the influences and the outlook that shaped Roland's intellectual development and scholarly career; it reflects the temperament and sense of proportion that have defined a long and useful life.

V. JACQUE VOEGELI

Acknowledgments

I wish to acknowledge the vital role of T. Michael Parrish of Baylor University and Sylvia Frank (now Sylvia Frank Rodrigue) of Louisiana State University Press in bringing this book into being. The three of us were at dinner at the annual convention of the Southern Historical Association in Little Rock when Mike broached the idea of my writing a life memoir and Sylvia seconded it. At first I didn't take it very seriously, but the more I thought about it the more attractive it became to me. So, working in my customary mode of fits and starts, I produced it and submitted it to Sylvia, to whom I am especially indebted for her patience and perseverance in negotiating the manuscript through the travails of review, evaluation, and revision. Without her efforts it would not have been published.

I wish to express my appreciation to Kent Masterson Brown for reading the manuscript in an early stage and encouraging me to submit it for publication; and to V. Jacque Voegeli of Vanderbilt University, Thomas H. Appleton of Eastern Kentucky University, Josephine Roland Riddick of Maury City, Tennessee, and Isaac N. and June Roland of Jackson, Tennessee, for reading it and offering helpful suggestions for its improvement. I wish also to thank those who read the manuscript anonymously for the Press. However irritated I may at first have been over their criticisms, I now see and acknowledge that they have markedly strengthened the book, and I am grateful for them. My thanks also to Gerry Anders of Louisiana State University Press for his patient and careful editing of the manuscript.

Finally, I wish to express my profound gratitude to my wife, Allie

Lee, who, as always, has been, to borrow from a popular song, "the wind beneath my wings." She had long urged me to write an account of my World War II experiences, and she has read every line of the present work (some of them several times) and offered invaluable comments for taming my wilder narrative impulses. In addition, she was obliged during the period of the revision of the manuscript to nurse me through my recovery from a heart attack and open-heart surgery. Her part in inspiring and sustaining me is beyond exaggeration.

Portions of this book have been drawn from two of my previously published works: "A Citizen Soldier Remembers World War II," in *Military Leadership and Command: The John Biggs Cincinnati Lectures, 1987,* presented here with the permission of the Virginia Military Institute Foundation, publisher; and "An American Soldier at the Bulge and at Remagen," in *World War II in Europe: The Final Year,* presented here with the permission of Brig. Gen. Charles F. Brower IV, U.S. Army (Retired), dean of the faculty, Virginia Military Institute, editor.

I am grateful also for the efforts of the McCormick Civil War Institute of Shenandoah University for its efforts in raising funds to support the publication of the photographs in the book. I wish to offer my sincere thanks to the individual donors for this purpose. They include: Pat Ashby; Tommy Barber; Brandon, Brian, and Kyle Beck; Winston Cameron Jr.; Jerrilynn Eby; Alan Fahring; John Fox; Richard Groome; Todd Kern; David Kerns; Charles and Martha Kirkpatrick; Jonathan Noyalas; Kenny Overby; Dorothy Overcash; Danny Powers; Steve Ritchie; Cecil Robinson; Bessie Solenberger; Eloise Strader; Melissa West; and Katherine Whitesell.

My Odyssey through History

In the Beginning

I was born April 8, 1918, in the little town of Maury City in western Tennessee. The event occurred, as I was later informed, in a small wooden house that stood on a street so undistinguished that the townspeople called it simply "the lane." Today, the street bears the name Park Avenue, an upgrading of nomenclature for which I am in no sense responsible.

My ancestry was respectable but neither wealthy nor famous. I am under the impression that my forebears were largely of Scotch-Irish stock. Some of my kinspeople have traced certain of them back to the late colonial period in North Carolina. Decades afterward they joined the great trek west and settled in southwestern Tennessee and northeastern Mississippi, where most of them have continued to live.

I came quite naturally by the urge to teach. Both my paternal grandfather and my father were teachers. My grandfather, Isaac Newton Roland, taught in a private high school in the rural community of Essary Springs, about seventy-five miles south of Maury City. According to all available accounts, he was a splendid instructor. During World War II, when I was stationed at a camp in Texas, I met an elderly man at church one Sunday. When we were introduced, he asked, "Are you akin to Professor I. N. Roland?" I explained the relationship. He revealed that he had been a pupil of my grandfather's in the Essary Springs school. Upon learning later that I planned to become a teacher after the war, he bestowed upon me this blessing: "I hope you will be as great a teacher as your grandfather was."

My grandfather met and married a student in the school, Mary Margaret Nelms, who became my grandmother. She was a tall and stately woman, and she held a strong sense of personal rectitude.

My father, Clifford Paul Roland, was the first of three children, all boys, born to the I. N. Rolands. He was born July 4, 1893. He was a healthy, handsome child. A photograph made when he was about two gives him a decidedly serious look. He would grow up to be a handsome man; a girlfriend of mine once told me that she and her friends agreed that none of my father's sons was as handsome as he. Somewhat crestfallen, I concurred. He was a generally serious and reserved man, but with a strong sense of humor and a deep love of life. He was highly intelligent and especially gifted in mathematics, and he was a conscientious student in all fields of learning. He was also a good athlete, particularly in basketball and baseball.

My maternal grandfather was Burton Paysinger. Born a few years before the Civil War, he retained fearful childhood memories of the conflict. He received only about two years of formal education, but this was sufficient to ground him far more thoroughly in reading, writing, and ciphering than are most high school graduates today. He acquired a lifelong love of words and was a natural orator and storyteller. He was fiery and impulsive. He was a cotton farmer and he served as a magistrate on the county court. He enjoyed whiskey and chewing tobacco.

My maternal grandmother's maiden name was Josephine Hurley. She was petite and, from my earliest memories of her, was quite hunched in the shoulders. She was quick of mind and tongue, and was said to have been a pretty girl and a light-footed dancer in her youth. We grandchildren called our Paysinger grandparents Ma and Pa because an older cousin had done so.

My mother, Grace Pearl Paysinger, was three years younger than my father. In her, I could see strong elements of both of her parents. She was pretty, bright, impulsive, and fiery. When she was about nine years old, the Paysingers sold their farm in McNairy County, Tennessee, and moved to Essary Springs in order that the children could attend the private school that was now being run by my grandfather Roland. My mother was a fast learner and soon caught up with all the pupils who had been ahead of her in her grade in school.

She first saw my father shortly after moving to Essary Springs. As she later put it, in meeting him she met her Waterloo. Apparently, they fell in love at first sight; they were married in 1916 after a long courtship. When my father walked down into the field where Pa Paysinger was plowing and asked for my mother's hand, Pa's only words were, "Well, Clifford, she's got a mighty high temper." The wedding was something of an early flower-child affair. Because one of my mother's sisters was seriously ill, the event could not take place in her home; instead, they met the presiding official by the roadside under a large oak tree where the ceremony occurred.

My father had attended a private college by the name of The National Teachers' Normal and Business College in the town of Henderson, Tennessee, which was on the Mobile and Ohio Railroad about thirty-five miles northeast of Essary Springs. He had been teaching school for two or three years in the village of Sardis, Tennessee, near the Tennessee River. He now accepted a position as co-principal of the high school in Maury City, about forty miles northwest of Henderson. He also coached the school's various athletics teams. My parents moved to Maury City shortly after their marriage. I was born there two years later; our family lived there until I was three.

My memories of life in Maury City are, of course, too dim to be reliable. According to community lore, one of the more sensational of these experiences occurred when I was an infant too young to remember it consciously. The story is that a teenaged girl engaged by my mother to babysit me had great difficulty stopping me from squalling. Finally, in desperation, she resorted to what the army would call a field expedient; she bared one breast and put me to it. I quieted instantly and was soon fast asleep. The experience may have affected me for life.

I do recall faintly some of the especially happy or especially painful episodes of my life there. For example: my parents playing the card game of Rook or eating homemade ice cream or watermelon with their friends, all the while engaged in laughter and lighthearted conversation; or an occasion when I inadvisably sampled the fiery-hot red peppers being grown in my mother's garden by the porch, an experience I was wise enough not to repeat.

In 1921 my family, which now included another son, Grady Paul, moved to Henderson, where my father had accepted a position on the faculty of Freed-Hardeman Junior College, the successor to The National Teachers' Normal and Business College. He would remain at Freed-Hardeman for the rest of his career. He retired from his service there on July 4, 1983, his ninetieth birthday. The school was affiliated with the Church of Christ. Most of the faculty were ministers in the church as well as teachers in the school, and in deciding to come there he decided also to enter the ministry.

My father's new position on the Freed-Hardeman faculty plus his role as a Church of Christ minister altered sharply the social and religious ambience surrounding the family. The college held a rather sternly puritanical outlook on life; it frowned on games of cards and on "mixed bathing," the term it applied to aquatic activities in which males and females swam together. Dancing was considered to be an unmitigated sin, one that would lead to horrendous lasciviousness. No longer did my parents engage in Rook parties; nor did they engage in any other social affairs except those related to the school, church, or family. The demands of the ministry caused my father to give up coaching. These restrictions and constraints would bear heavily on me as I grew older.

I went through the usual experiences of a young child in a small southern town of that era. I survived the severe childhood diseases that were popularly known as whooping cough and red measles, and the relatively mild diseases known as chicken pox and German measles. I had the best medical attention available at the time, but the best could be taxing. It included, for example, an annual purging. Every spring, our family physician would prescribe a "round of calomel to clear out the system," which had to be followed by a dose of castor oil. This procedure did indeed clear out the system! This occurred whether or not there were any symptoms that would have justified the ordeal, which seemed to me to be worse than any condition it might have cured or averted. All members of my family also faithfully took quinine to ward off malaria.

In Henderson, the Roland family grew with the addition of a daughter, Margaret Josephine (namesake of both grandmothers), Hall Carmack, and Isaac Nelms. I loved my siblings but seemed to be compelled to bedevil the two of them nearest my age. I once got Josephine (Jo for short) up on top of the house by way of a ladder that someone had carelessly left in place. I was unable to get her down, and my parents were not immediately available. Fortunately, a passing college student rescued her.

I constantly provoked fights with Paul. I also led him into all sorts of mischief. The very first words of every Henderson acquaintance of mine when encountered in later years were: "You and Paul were the worst kids I ever knew." In my maturity I have come to believe that jealousy was the cause of my picking on Paul. He had replaced me as the baby of the family. Also, he was more attractive than I. He possessed a round face with cheeks like big red apples; my face was sharp and pale by comparison. Invariably, some of the first words spoken when the family visited relatives were: "Isn't Paul cute?" Then, turning to me, "I do declare. Charles looks a little peaked, doesn't he?"

Josephine, five years my junior, posed a different kind of threat to my security. She was a girl. I soon began to derive great pleasure out of teasing her. She was a perfect target because she reacted so predictably and in a manner so gratifying to me. I honed my teasing talents to the point that I could send her screeching out of the room merely with a gesture or a knowing glance in her direction. I once appropriated her menu for a party she was planning for herself and her girlfriends. The menu called for a dime's worth of candy and seventeen glasses of cocoa-malt, a favorite family beverage that was thought to possess marvelous health-promoting qualities. The mention of that menu fifty years later would send her into blushes and gales of embarrassed laughter.

I entered the Freed-Hardeman elementary school at age five. For a long time afterward, I believed my parents started me early because of my precocity. After I became a parent, I began to suspect they were motivated at least in part by the need to get me out of the house for a while each day. Unquestionably, they had good cause for wanting to do this.

I was definitely not a good pupil. There is little doubt that today I would be diagnosed as being hyperactive; I had certain twitches and motions that may have been symptoms of what is now identified as Tourette's syndrome. To say that I had an attention deficit would be a gross understatement; I had an attention void. In all probability, I would today be put on medication. I was indescribably bored with most of my classes, notwithstanding that my teacher was a quite pretty young woman who was just out of college and who aroused in me all sorts of unidentifiable sensations.

I was unable, or unwilling, to memorize the information required by the tests. Arithmetic was a profound mystery to me. My lack of aptitude in the field is still a mystery to me, since both of my parents and all of my siblings were especially good in it. Fortunately, reading came easy for me. Also, both my teacher and my classmates gave me high marks for my ability as a narrator or raconteur, though these activities often got me into trouble for talking when I should have been silent.

Girls presented a serious distraction. They seemed to be the repositories of all beauty and brains. The ancient saying that little girls are made of sugar and spice and everything nice, and little boys of snaps and snails and puppy dog tails, I accepted as eternal verities. The girls came to school in immaculate dresses and shiny patent-leather shoes, their hair done in flawless braids or curls. The contrast between their appearance and mine was too painful for contemplation. One day while in the first grade I slipped up on a golden-haired little angel and stole a kiss; she ran home to her mother in tears. I felt like the troll who had emerged from under the bridge.

The intellectual contrast was as striking as the physical one. The little girls almost always got their tests back with big red 100s marked on them. They were downcast when they received a 99. If I had received a grade that high I would have known somebody had shuffled the papers.

Corporal punishment, both at home and in school, was a prevalent condition of growing up when I was young. In my early years my parents whipped with switches; later, my father whipped with his belt. There were periods when I was whipped at least once a day, some days, more than once. "Spare the rod, spoil the child" was the accepted wisdom in parenting. Strangely, despite the present view that such practice constitutes child abuse and inflicts permanent psychological trauma, I never felt abused, never ceased to love my parents, never questioned their love for me. Whether the experience crushed or otherwise dismembered my personality, I leave to others. How much effect the punishment had on my behavior at the time is debatable.

In addition to the whippings at home, I was also whipped quite often in school. Yet I continued to misbehave regularly both places. When I was a teenager I received lashings at school hard enough to leave stripes that were clearly visible across my back for days when I was swimming with my cohorts. I wore the stripes as proudly as an army sergeant wears those on his chevron.

I was wounded by one of Cupid's arrows while in my early teens. My first actual romantic encounter occurred in the unlikely environs of the Freed-Hardeman College tennis courts. I found myself by accident in close proximity to a charming, sloe-eyed young brunette of about my own age. Before I knew it, we were embracing, kissing. To my utter bewilderment, she suddenly disengaged and fled, leaving me in a state of suspended animation.

Notwithstanding the frequency of domestic punishments, I can see that I was blessed with a secure and bounteous home. I never wanted for nourishing food or comfortable clothing and housing. There were always toys and other gifts at Christmas. This was possible during the Great Depression of the early thirties because Freed-Hardeman College resorted to barter in lieu of nonexistent cash; the faculty accepted goods and produce from parents in payment of their children's tuition fees. Also, in our home there was always parental love, albeit of a painful application on countless occasions.

Speaking of Christmas, in the Church of Christ it was an altogether secular occasion. We shot fireworks on Christmas the way most Americans elsewhere shot them on the Fourth of July. The bombardment began weeks in advance and gradually reached fortissimo on Christmas Day. By dawn that morning the town of Henderson sounded somewhat like the battle of Gettysburg.

In spite of my unimpressive performance in school, I managed to acquire an acceptable knowledge of the basics in education. My formal schooling was immensely reinforced by reading and by a certain amount of travel. When I was seven or eight my parents purchased a second-hand set of the youths' encyclopedia named *The Book of Knowledge*. Its many volumes (thirty, as I recall) contained snippets of almost every imaginable branch of literature and learning. Through the years I may have read every word of the entire work.

I also had ready access to a set of world classics that my father owned and kept in his home library. They were published in separate little volumes. Admittedly, they were a bit mature for me, but I read many of them anyway, including Homer's *Iliad* and *Odyssey*. Such of their expressions as "rosy-fingered dawn" and "wine-dark sea" struck a responsive chord in me. I read with intense satisfaction how the suitors of the wife of the absent and wandering Ulysses, pretending to be Ulysses, failed the test of identity to which they were subjected. Only Ulysses could draw the bow of Ulysses.

Another important source of my intellectual development lay in certain of the popular novels of the time. I devoured the novels of Zane Grey telling of the exploits of bold western riders and the Tarzan novels of Edgar Rice Burroughs with their story of a muscular young superman who was reared by the great anthropoid apes of Africa.

Unquestionably, the supreme literary influence on my youth was the King James Bible, in which I did a considerable amount of obligatory reading, but which came to me primarily through quotations—innumerable, reiterated quotations in sermons, Sunday school classes, and Freed-Hardeman's compulsory daily chapel exercises. After almost eight decades many of these striking passages still ring in my mind: "The heavens declare the glory of God and the firmament sheweth his handiwork"; "Consider the lilies of the field, how they grow; they toil not, neither do they spin: And yet . . . Solomon in all his glory was not arrayed like one of these."

An unintended enhancement in my early formal education—a piece of serendipity—was the result of the presence in the Freed-Hardeman elementary and high school of a number of pupils from a wide portion of the nation, including such faraway and exotic regions as Florida, Illinois, and Texas, as well as such closer places as the cities of Nashville and Memphis. What I did not understand at the time but have come to believe is that at least some of them were there to receive a discipline that their parents were unable or unwilling to exercise at home. In other words, Freed-Hardeman served them somewhat as a reform school. Hence, among them were a number of previously undisciplined and highly mischievous (if not miscreant) boys and girls. They lived in the college dormitories, thus further developing their questionable knowledge and skills by contact with the older residents. All of this gave the Freed-Hardeman lower schools an extraordinary degree of versatility, energy, and color.

I profited immensely from these associations, though my parents would have been horrified by a lot of what I was learning. The most memorable of these youthful boarding pupils was a boy named Baskin Fuller (nicknamed Bosey) from Florida. Bosey was four or five years older than I. He was handsome, bright, articulate, and altogether charming; he probably grew up to be a highly successful lawyer, doctor, engineer, or business executive. He was also the quintessential corrupting influence according to the accepted Freed-Hardeman (or Roland household) point of view. He possessed a seemingly inexhaustible stock of gamy jokes and stories, and an equally ample repertory of sexual information (and misinformation) that he generously passed on to all of his youthful acquaintances. Since I received virtually no information on this subject at home, I looked to Bosey as my tutor in the course.

When I was in the seventh grade it was merged with the eighth grade because of the smallness of the enrollment in both at Freed-Hardeman. As a result, I went through both seventh and eighth grades in a single year. I was able to handle this speed-up all right in everything but arithmetic, where I had always been weak.

There was another result of the speed-up: I would graduate from high school just a month after turning sixteen years of age. This would put me into college about two years younger than most of my associates there, thus placing me at a social disadvantage because of my relative immaturity.

I was greatly stimulated by the visits our family made to places of historical interest and societal importance. By all odds the place that left the greatest impression on me was Shiloh. In the days when there were virtually no public recreation areas, the National Military Park commemorating the great Civil War battle that occurred there, and located only an hour's drive from my home, was a favorite spot for visiting. I went there on countless family or school occasions. I picked up Civil War musket bullets from the ground. I once startled a colleague mildly by saying that I may have made my very first trip to Shiloh before I was born.

Shiloh, of course, was more than just a recreation area. It was the site of an episode of immense tragic historic significance. The scores of cannons and monuments scattered across the fields and throughout the woods offered striking testimony to the events that occurred there. The place was hallowed ground to me. I drank in its historic scenes, the Hornets' Nest, the Sunken Road, the Peach Orchard, the Bloody Pond; I listened in awe to the saga of valor describing the fray. I stood under the great white oak tree where Gen. Albert Sidney Johnston, the Confederate commander, was found mortally wounded, and I listened to my grandfather say that Johnston's death had robbed the Confederates of victory there, perhaps of victory in the war. How could anyone, including me, know as I sat at age eight or nine for a Freed-Hardeman College group photograph on the Johnston monument that I would one day write the story of his life.

The other family visits that ranked almost with Shiloh in my consciousness were the annual Essary Springs community reunions. Hundreds of people came from hundreds of miles; a din of animated conversation and laughter floated over the place; mountains of food lay on rustic wooden tables under the trees; a constant line of people dipped and drank water from the spring (Essary Spring) that flowed into the Hatchie River a few feet away. We drank the water as a social ritual even when we were not the least thirsty; drank it until we were waterlogged and forced to seek relief wherever. Youngsters shot marbles and played ball; youths flirted and courted; the older folk told and retold stories of family, church, and community. The entire event was one of hearty bucolic conviviality.

My early years were lived without benefit of the so-called "miracle" drugs that would become prevalent during and following World War II. Fortunately, I inherited a body that was resistant enough to be spared all of the dread diseases of the period, such as polio, tuberculosis, meningitis, typhoid fever, scarlet fever, and the like. I had friends who died or were permanently disabled or weakened by one or another of these maladies.

My early years were also lived without benefit of organized athletics for children. We boys learned to swim by trial and error in a little nearby stream that bore the suggestive name Sugar Creek. Throughout its normal course the creek was perhaps twenty feet wide and two feet deep. But here and there were holes as much as seven or eight feet deep that served us admirably as swimming pools. Though I have been privileged to swim in many elaborate artificial pools, in both the Atlantic Ocean and the Pacific Ocean, in the Gulf of Mexico, Lake Pontchartrain, Lake Michigan, and the beautiful Barton Springs near Austin, Texas, I have never had greater aquatic pleasure than I enjoyed in muddy little Sugar Creek.

We wore no swimsuits. We "skinny dipped," shedding our scanty summer clothes as we raced the last few hundred feet to the creek and shouted, "Last one in is a [whatever insult or epithet came to mind]." One of our keenest pleasures occurred in a swimming hole that was close to the trestle bridge where the railroad crossed the stream. We "flashed" the passing passenger trains shamelessly. Startled women looked with open-mouthed indignation, startled girls with open-mouthed amusement. Between swims and flashing the trains, we re-enacted the Tarzan story in a thick woods that grew along the creek bank. Still nude as at the moment of birth, we swung like monkeys from tree to tree, emitting the high-pitched, triumphal cries of our hero.

We played baseball, basketball, and football on vacant lots and in nearby cow pastures. We chose sides in a procedure that was explicitly and humiliatingly based on merit; the self-appointed captain of each team selected his players according to a descending scale of ability. The boy who was by general agreement the weakest baseball player in town happened to own most of the baseball equipment, including bats, balls, and a catcher's mask, mitt, and body protector. Though we had to allow him to play in order to get the use of the equipment, he was invariably chosen last, and with the proviso that the captain be permitted to take his last strike at bat.

As I grew older I played on the Freed-Hardeman high school and college teams. I was the Henderson boys' tennis champion (sixteen and under), and my partner and I were the town senior doubles champions though I was still young enough to qualify for the boys' competition. I was the number two player on the college tennis team. In football I was known as a "scatback," a light but swift and shifty runner. I played safety on defense, which meant that I returned the other team's punts. I have a distinct and scary memory of skipping around and watching the ball as it floated and wobbled high in the air above me, at the same time listening to the rumble of the big, beefy opposition players as they bore down on me like a herd of buffalo. In baseball I was a pitcher, with a local reputation of throwing a "fire-ball." One of my dearest friends later in life accused me of intimidating the batters by throwing the first pitch dangerously close to their heads.

In order to supplement the family income at the height of the Great Depression, my father decided to convert the five-acre plot of land on which we lived into a vegetable and fruit farm and dairy. He also had a nonfinancial motive in doing this. Reared on a farm and steeped in the Jeffersonian philosophy that those who work in the soil with their hands are God's chosen people, he hoped to develop his children's characters in this manner. As teenagers, Paul and I ran the dairy, milking five cows apiece by hand, and carrying out the many other chores that went along with the enterprise. We also delivered the raw milk to customers after our mother had strained and bottled it.

We cultivated the small farm during the summer under an arrangement that we would work every morning and have the afternoons free to swim or play tennis or baseball. I could say what Abraham Lincoln is quoted as having said: that my father taught me how to work, but not how to enjoy it. Whether these activities enhanced our characters I cannot say, but they developed our muscles and probably kept us out of a degree of mischief.

I particularly relished visiting with one of my Corinth, Mississippi, aunts, who was the mother of three vivacious daughters in my general age range. I traveled back and forth from Henderson on a single-coach diesel-electric train known locally as the Dinky. My cousins imparted to me many social virtues, and some of what were looked upon in my family circle as social vices. They taught me how to dance the Charleston, sort of. The choreography occurred in a most unlikely place: the bandstand of a renowned Civil War battle site, Battery Robinett of the battle of Corinth. The lessons were accompanied by rhythmic chanting and handclapping and sometimes by the jazz music of a portable windup phonograph.

As all of us grew older, our escapades grew more daring. I took my first drink of alcohol, a minimal sip of beer, in company with the three cousins and the boyfriends of the two eldest. This took place at a rustic beer joint just across the Tennessee line, because Mississippi was "dry," while beer was allowed in Tennessee. Many years later State Line, Tennessee, with a cluster of disreputable establishments allegedly featuring gambling and prostitution, would become the locale of violence in the popular movie *Walking Tall*.

When I was about fifteen the youngest of the cousins, who was approximately my own age, began to arrange dates for me with her girlfriends. She coached me in advance concerning my upcoming date's qualifications, tastes, and whims. My visits to Corinth were filled with excitement and fun.

My first two years of college were spent at Freed-Hardeman. I was an indifferent student as a freshman, barely managing to pass the required mathematics courses, earning C's in most courses, and no grade higher than a B. Mainly, I studied girls, all of whom were older than I and seemed far more sophisticated. My scores weren't very high in that subject either.

In the fall of my second year something happened that brought a significant change in my life. I was sitting with a group of local friends of mine on the courthouse yard evaluating the girls as they came and went to the soda fountain of the City Drug Store across the street. A discussion of college came up. One friend said he was headed for Duke, another for the University of Alabama, one for "Ole Miss" (the University of Mississippi), several for the University of Tennessee. Someone turned to me, addressed me by my nickname, "Chick," and asked where I intended to go to school after graduating from Freed-Hardeman. I had not given the matter a thought, but I felt called upon to offer an answer in order to save face. Because my father had attended Vanderbilt to do graduate work, that school popped into my mind. "I'll be going to Vanderbilt," I replied archly.

The more I thought of that possibility, the more the idea appealed to me. That evening at the dinner table (we called the evening meal "supper") I suddenly announced my intention to attend Vanderbilt. This statement was followed by a long silence, but afterward my father sat me down for a solemn talk about my future. He pledged to find the means to send me to Vanderbilt if that was where I wished to go, then he added another condition. "Provided," he said, "Vanderbilt will accept you." The thought that I might not be accepted had not entered my mind. He explained forcefully that my Freed-Hardeman record up to that point would not be acceptable. That evening, for the first time ever,

I began studying seriously. According to my memory, I received nothing but A's for the remainder of my Freed-Hardeman career.

Vanderbilt did accept me, though I have wondered at times whether the decision may not have been influenced by my father's position and associations, including his being a Vanderbilt alumnus, and in September 1936 I enrolled there. As events turned out, I found myself to be quite adequately prepared educationally for the Vanderbilt experience. French was the course that I was most anxious about. Had my year of studying the language at a small junior college equipped me for an advanced university course in it? My anxiety increased when the instructor at Vanderbilt turned out to be a native Frenchman. To determine whether all of the students were qualified for the course, he administered a test at the first class meeting. To my delight and incredulity, he announced at the next meeting that the highest score on the test was that of Monsieur Roland. This gave me a tremendous boost in morale (and egotism); never again did I doubt my ability to do acceptable work at Vanderbilt. My score in French was actually a tribute to my Freed-Hardeman instructor in the language, Mrs. Mary Nelle Hardeman Powers, an extraordinarily intelligent and inspiring teacher.

Notwithstanding my recently acquired self-confidence, the university intellectual atmosphere was extremely rarefied for my system. In evaluating my Freed-Hardeman courses for acceptance, a brisk young woman in the Vanderbilt dean's office told me that only a portion of my Bible courses would receive credit and that the credit would count in lieu of "Bib Lit" (Biblical Literature). What I had studied as the inerrant revealed Word of God was thus transformed in the twinkling of an eye into nine quarter hours of "Bib Lit"! My course in the history of the American frontier, taught by the department chairman, Professor William C. Binkley, was a genuine eye-opener. I had always studied history as a body of fixed facts. Exposed to Frederick Jackson Turner's "frontier hypothesis" (that the American frontier experience had given the nation a unique character) and to my professor's commentary on the hypothesis, I learned to examine all historical "facts" critically and through a set of corrective lenses.

Vanderbilt offered me an excellent education, and I profited immensely from it. A number of professors, in addition to Dr. Binkley, are especially memorable. Frank Owsley was my major adviser, and I took his splendid course in the history of sectional controversy. Donald Davidson and John Crowe Ransom stood in on many occasions for the instructor in one of my courses in English literature.

In studying under these three professors, I was being exposed to some of the most brilliant, creative, and controversial scholars in the nation. Davidson and Ransom were members of the celebrated group of southern writers who called themselves "The Fugitives" and were leaders in the school of literary interpretation known as the New Criticism, which placed its decisive emphasis on form, structure, paradox, and imagery. Owsley, one of the most distinguished and original of all historians of the South, had joined Ransom, Davidson, and a number of other thinkers who in 1930, under the group name "Twelve Southerners" (widely known as "The Agrarians"), published the book *I'll Take My Stand*. It was a southern literary manifesto against the progressive, industrialized society that they deplored as a threat to the southern way of life, the environment of the entire earth, and universal classical values. Ransom captured the philosophy of the book brilliantly in a single sentence in the preface that described the modern progressive society as being constantly engaged in a losing war with nature, "winning Pyrrhic victories at points of no strategic importance."

Was I aware of the privilege of sitting at the feet of these men? Not in the slightest. I admired them as interesting classroom teachers and I liked them personally, but I was too ignorant to be cognizant of their importance as intellectuals. I was also too callow to care. Not until I was a graduate student a decade of years and a world of experiences later did I come to appreciate them for what they were.

My social education at Vanderbilt was fully as important as my intellectual education. Measured by the standards of campus life of the time, the school and its student body were decidedly conservative; measured by today's standards, they represented the Stone Age. The boys were clean-shaven and wore neckties to class. The girls came to class looking like dolls—modest dolls, for they wore knee-length skirts and hose that exposed no flesh beneath the hem of the skirt. The prime enforcer of the girls' dress code was Dean of Women Ada Belle Stapleton. She cut a formidable figure. A woman of imposing height and girth, she had the eye of an eagle and the tongue of an adder. She was known to order girls back to their rooms to don the proper attire, or to remove exactly half of their rouge and lipstick. She was also known to stop boys on the campus who failed to tip their hats to her and have them do so "by the numbers." A hippie among the Vanderbilt students of the day would have been as unimaginable as a Bolshevik.

I had two great summers during my college career. The first was between my sophomore and junior years (before going to Vanderbilt) when I served as a counselor at a boys camp—Camp Elklore—in the beautiful hilly and wooded country near the town of Winchester in Middle Tennessee. In addition to being in charge of a cabin housing ten or twelve young teenagers, I taught tennis and swimming. Between my junior and senior college years I held a summer job with the National Park Service, working as a guide at the Chickamauga-Chattanooga National Battlefield Park. I loved both of the summers' experiences.

I was a middling good student at Vanderbilt, with grades about half A's and half B's. After proving to myself the first year that I was capable of making A's in French, I eased back to a comfortable B in the language. My proudest moments came during the senior seminar my last year. Professor Owsley was in charge of the American history quarter of the course. For it I wrote a research paper on the battles for Chattanooga during the Civil War. Since I had served throughout the preceding summer as a guide in these battlefields and had given countless lectures on the campaign, writing this seminar paper was "a piece of cake." I received a grade of A on it.

Writing the paper for the European quarter of the course was a different matter. Not only had I not been a guide or lecturer on any European topic; the instructor in the course was a Professor Cruikshank, who was known to be a particularly severe grader. I had been happy over eking out a modest B in his lecture course. From his list of acceptable seminar topics, I chose one on the Norman conquest of the Sicilies, about which I knew nothing. I worked on it throughout the entire quarter, collecting bits of information wherever the reference librarian and I could find them. I turned in the paper in a quite diffident mood; a grade of B would have made me decidedly happy. Instead, I received an A and was told by the professor that mine was the superior paper of the seminar. I went away rejoicing.

My social life was much freer at Vanderbilt than at Freed-Hardeman. I became a dedicated dancer, began to imbibe alcohol in strict moderation, and to smoke cigarettes accordingly. Because my funds for social purposes were extremely limited, I did not date Vanderbilt girls—who, I understood, expected to be wined and dined. Instead, I dated girls who were in school at Peabody College across the street from Vanderbilt; they were training to become schoolteachers and expected less to be spent on them. I also dated high school girls, who were delighted to be brought to the Student Union dances held periodically in the gymnasium.

It was my good fortune to form a friendship with a student who was destined to become one of the nation's most popular celebrities. Her name was Fanny Rose Shore; she became the radio, movie, and TV singing star Dinah Shore. I knew who she was before I met her directly. Everybody on campus knew Fanny Rose, knew her as an attractive, outgoing, friendly, and talented young woman. She sang on a weekly program of a local radio station. She and I were enrolled in a large Political Science course in which the professor seated the students alphabetically. This arrangement put the two of us side by side on the back row and we quickly became classroom buddies.

One day she said to me, "I saw you playing tennis. Would you teach me to play tennis?" Would I teach her? You can bet I would! We made a date and I reserved a campus court. I was utterly intimidated by her appearance on the court. I played tennis in an ordinary pair of wash trousers and a street shirt with its sleeves cut off and hemmed by my mother. She appeared in tennis attire de rigueur, carrying a fancy tennis equipment bag with an expensive racquet and a can of fresh tennis balls. Once we were on the court, I saw immediately that someone else had beaten me to the job of teaching her how to play the game. We played on a few subsequent occasions, but her social calendar was too busy for such a casual arrangement to last very long.

An amusing incident occurred between us at the end of the Political Science course. One of the course requirements was the preparation of a research term paper. Near the close of the term she confided to me exultantly that she had recently interviewed the governor of Tennessee as a part of her research. My own work seemed to me to be awfully pedestrian compared with such a spectacular feat. On the day the papers were to be turned in she said to me, "Let me see your paper. Here's mine." We exchanged papers. After just enough time for her to scan my opening paragraph, she returned my paper with the exclamation, "My God! I'm not even gonna turn mine in!" She did turn hers in and probably received a good grade on it, for she was a quite competent student. We graduated together in the spring of 1938.

I was happy to be out of college, because I was tired of school work. But I still had little awareness of the realities of life. I took for granted that my parents would continue to support me. For a while they did. To acquire a modest amount of spending money I took a job that summer lifeguarding at Chickasaw State Park near Henderson. I also continued to live at home, eat most of my meals there, and drive my parents' automobile when I needed wheels, including the frequent occasions when I was on dates either with Henderson girls or with girls in the nearby town of Jackson.

One day my father casually informed me that he had spoken to a friend in Memphis who was the district sales manager for a national life insurance company. They had discussed my gifts as a salesman, and he had assured my father that I amply possessed the qualifications for such a career. Suddenly I could see dollar signs floating before my eyes, along with a wardrobe of modish attire and an automobile of sleek design, possibly a Terraplane like that of one of my friends. I signed a formidable contract and began diligently studying sales manuals and forms. This was an easy task after the taxing reading demands of my college courses. I continued to live at home and freeload off my parents.

I soon discovered that actually selling insurance was quite different from reading about selling it. In college I had been articulate, some would say loquacious, in discussing my coursework; now I felt embarrassed and tongue-tied when I attempted to explain the advantages of my product to an impatient potential customer. Two months went by without a sale except two small policies purchased by my father: one for my brother and one for me. I began to entertain serious doubts about my ability to do this kind of work; eventually, I quit trying to make sales and began sitting at home in an attitude of defeat.

Again my father came to my rescue. He set me on a course that ultimately would be my life's work.

A Budding Career

One day in late September or early October 1938, my father learned that the high school in Alamo, Tennessee, was in search of a history teacher. He suggested that we look into the situation. Sick of my barren insurance job, I heartily agreed.

Through his foresight and urging, I held a certificate entitling me to teach three subjects (history, English, and French) in the state's public elementary and secondary schools. In order to acquire the certificate I had enrolled while in college in all but one of the courses required for certification. The one I had skipped was perhaps the most important of all: Practice Teaching. Astonishingly, my father had also taken care of this deficit. One summer he had hired me to teach a freshman United States history course in Freed-Hardeman College. He now managed to persuade the state Department of Education to accept this experience in lieu of Practice Teaching. I suspect this arrangement was facilitated by the circumstance that the state commissioner of education was a distant relative of my mother's, and his son and I had graduated together from Vanderbilt, where we had been casual friends.

Alamo is located about forty miles northwest of my hometown. It is in Crockett County and is only about five miles from my birthplace, Maury City, where my father had been principal of the high school and had served as superintendent of the county schools. Probably helped by these circumstances, I got the job.

I taught in the Alamo high school for two full school years and began a third. I had always heard that teaching school is a valuable life experience. But I had always wondered, "Valuable for what?" Only after many additional years of life did I come to a partial answer to this question.

No doubt, I did significantly enhance my knowledge of the information in the courses that I taught. I had heard also that a teacher learns more about a subject than his students learn. I am convinced that this held true for me. Perhaps as much out of personal vanity—the desire to be admired—as out of a determination to improve the students' minds, I worked hard to prepare myself for the courses.

In order to be brilliant, or appear to be, I virtually memorized the lessons in the textbooks, then I attempted to enrich my lectures and discussions by reading books and articles beyond the textbook. At first I felt pretty shaky in standing up before a classroom full of seventeen- and eighteen-year-olds, but I soon became comfortable with it. Though I had little appreciation of the ultimate value of the experience, in developing my ability to communicate verbally with the students I was developing one of the most important skills of life.

I learned much also from my associations with the students outside the classroom. I suspect I learned more from them collectively than they learned from me. I was only twenty years old when I began teaching. Many of my students were almost as old as I; a few were actually older. Shortly after I began teaching, my principal, a man by the unlikely name T. Happle Strange, offered me some valuable avuncular advice. He warned me against the temptation to become socially involved (especially amorously involved) with any of the female students. "You may admire them, if you wish," he said, "but don't go out with any of them. And especially don't touch any of them." The advice was excellent, and I heeded it punctiliously; I observed and admired, but neither dated nor touched.

The time I spent teaching in Alamo saw the peak of the big-band era in American popular music. It came just as the electric phonograph (the "jukebox") had been perfected. It also coincided with the development of high-speed family automobiles such as the V-8 Ford, and the appearance of new, paved roads suited to them. This combination of factors caused a proliferation of highway nightclubs throughout the country.

On any Friday or Saturday night in any one of a number of favorite clubs scattered across West Tennessee, one could expect to find acquaintances from a number of towns socializing and dancing to the jukebox tunes of the nationally famous bands of Guy Lombardo, Sammy Kaye, Glen Miller, Benny Goodman, or others. Club hopping, going from one to another on the same evening, was a favorite sport. I participated enthusiastically in these activities. I recall one occasion when three couples of us, on a lark, visited clubs in three different states in one night, beginning at Corinth in northern Mississippi, traversing West Tennessee, and ending across the state line in Kentucky.

Memphis, seventy miles west of Henderson, was the social Mecca of the area. Two or three times each summer we would make a pilgrimage there, going in a small cavalcade of automobiles, sometimes picking up dates in towns along the way. We danced at the pavilion on the roof of the Peabody Hotel to the music of one or another of the nation's celebrity bands. I first heard the "champagne" rhythms of Lawrence Welk's band there in the summer of 1939 or 1940.

During the summer of 1939, I returned to Henderson and lived with my parents. I again worked as a lifeguard at the nearby Chickasaw State Park. This was decidedly more play than work, and it allowed us lifeguards to meet unattached girls from a wide area. After the swimming period ended at night, we danced to the jukebox in the park lodge or drove into Henderson to the ice plant, where we obtained cold watermelons which we cut and ate at our convenience. We did, on occasion, save someone from drowning in the lake.

My teaching job was my first regular salaried employment. Quite naturally, it gave me a certain feeling of having "arrived." For the first time, I had a bank account, albeit an extremely modest one. A friend of mine who worked as an assistant cashier in the Bank of Alamo would kid me about the amounts written on my checks: frequently no more than one or two dollars.

To place these meager sums in perspective, however, I need to point out that they would then purchase many times what they purchase today. The nation was still in the grip of the Great Depression, and all salaries and financial figures reflected this situation. My salary during my first year of teaching was sixty dollars per month; the following year it was elevated to seventy dollars. Moreover, a portion of the salary was paid in county school warrants which were only theoretically redeemable in cash. In other words, the county government did not have the money to redeem them. Local merchants accepted them in lieu of cash but at a sharp discount from the face value.

The unmarried teachers boarded in the homes of town families. All of the women teachers boarded in this way, because they were forbidden to be married. I have never understood the logic of this prohibition; it seemed to me that it encouraged them to engage in some of the very activities it was intended to prevent. I shared a room with another man. My board, including three meals a day, cost thirty dollars per month.

The people of Alamo, including the other teachers, were extraordinarily hospitable and kind to me. The school principal became a warm friend of mine and gave me many pieces of worthwhile counsel in addition to that about how to conduct myself with the female pupils.

During a part of the summer of 1940 I taught Business English (a combination of grammar and composition for the writing of letters and reports) in a business school in Florence, Alabama. Many of the students were badly in need of language instruction. I did the best I could with them and hoped I was successful.

The proprietress of the school, a Mrs. Larimore, was a dear friend of my parents. She had for many years taught business courses at Freed-Hardeman. I had known her since I was about three years old. I remembered her with affection because once when I was about ten years old and she was serving as the mistress of the dining room in the girls' dormitory, she had invited me to dinner there and seated me next to a pretty coed whose presence left me breathless.

I lived during the summer of 1940 in the home of Mrs. Larimore and her husband. It was a large plantation-style house in a beautiful wooded area a few miles outside Florence. The atmosphere of the house was made decidedly more exciting by the presence of the proprietress's attractive eighteen-year-old niece, Doris. The experience of living there was made exciting also by the presence in the neighborhood of a family named Moore, whose son was married to Doris's elder sister. The Moores lived in a gracious house set back several hundred feet from the road behind a deep and broad lot of large oaks and other hardwood trees. In the middle of the lot was a spring of sparkling water surrounded by picnic tables that served as the setting of frequent cook-outs called "bacon fries" because they featured mounds of crisply fried bacon and slices of tomatoes, onions, and pickles, along with hamburger buns. No food ever tasted better.

I quickly formed a warm friendship with a younger Moore son, James, who was a student at the state college that was located in Florence. He was bright and handsome and was well acquainted with a covey of charming coeds. The two of us expended a considerable amount of energy entertaining these young women. My association with Jim Moore would be renewed thirty years later when I joined the faculty of the University of Kentucky, where he had been teaching for a number of years. He and his wife, Margaret, became two of the dearest Kentucky friends of my wife and me.

While I was teaching in Alamo, affairs from the outer world began to intrude ominously into my life and the lives of all Americans. While in college, through the influence of some of my professors, I had become keenly interested in the volatile European situation. I had at the time read treatises on Karl Marx's communist analysis of society and had read his and Engels's book *The Communist Manifesto*. But the work I had read that most intrigued and alarmed me was Adolph Hitler's *Mein Kampf*. I was convinced that another war was in the offing, and in 1939 it erupted. I devoured the war news as it poured out from the press and radio.

The collapse of France shook me severely. The desperate plight of England disturbed me even more; my sympathy for the people of that country under heavy aerial bombardment was profound; my admiration for the handful of dauntless British airmen who fought off the Luftwaffe was boundless. Prime Minister Winston Churchill's immortal tribute to them stirred me to the quick. "Never in the field of human conflict was so much owed by so many to so few." His ringing assertion of indomitable British defiance had a similar effect on me. He vowed that the British population would fight the Nazis on the sea and in the air, on the beaches, in the fields and in the streets, and in the hills. "We shall not flag or fail. . . . We shall never surrender."

When in September 1940 the United States adopted conscription, I approved of the measure, though I was not thrilled at the thought of serving in the armed forces and gave a sigh of relief over having drawn a high number in the draft. I would have quite a stretch of time left before being called up.

I returned to Alamo in the fall of 1940 and resumed teaching in the high school. About a month into the session my life suddenly took an unexpected and dramatic turn. Two years earlier, on my father's advice, I had taken a civil service examination for a job as a historian in government service. Doubtless, a report on my score was sent to me, though I do not recall such. Weeks, months, years passed with no further word.

Then, just as I was settling into my third year of teaching, a telegram informed me that I had been appointed to a position of historical aide in the National Park Service and assigned to the National Capital Parks in Washington, D.C., at an annual salary of $1,440. This was electrifying news. Here was an opportunity to see the world far beyond the confines of my previous life and be paid what seemed to me at the time a handsome sum for doing so.

I promptly resigned the teaching job, though with pangs of regret, for I had enjoyed both it and the friends I had made in Alamo. Also, I regretted leaving a comely young woman colleague I had begun dating that fall. But almost immediately the excitement of the thought of living in the nation's capital blotted out these emotions.

Returning briefly to Henderson, I purchased myself a new wardrobe, bade my family and friends there goodbye, and rode the Dinky to Corinth, where I boarded a Southern Railway train for Washington. The trip took almost twenty-four hours, which I passed sitting up in the day coach and catching brief naps as I could.

We pulled into the great Washington station in the middle of the morning. I rode a trolley to the home of some family friends who had been students at Freed-Hardeman. The ride was unforgettable. It took us past the Capitol and the White House, and in full view of the towering Washington Monument. The scenes were enchanting beyond words; here was the city beautiful.

My job turned out to be a fascinating one. It rotated from place to place within the Capital parks, including the Lincoln Museum (located in Ford's Theater where the renowned president was assassinated), the Lincoln Memorial, the Washington Monument, and the Lee Mansion in

Arlington Cemetery overlooking Washington from across the Potomac River. My duties involved delivering brief lectures to the visitors to these sites. The lectures included information about both the memorials themselves and the figures they memorialized. At first I pretty much recited canned talks provided by the Park Service, but I worked to enrich my lectures by additional study, and my experience as a teacher now proved to be invaluable.

I went about my duties with genuine sincerity, an attitude that came easily from the very nature of the places where I worked. Frivolity would have been entirely out of order in such a place as the mansion where Lee had lived or the theater where Lincoln was shot. Or before the great brooding form of Lincoln in the memorial that bears his name.

Social life in Washington was strikingly different from that in the small towns of Tennessee. Neither I nor any of my acquaintances in Washington owned or had access to an automobile. We were obliged to ride trolleys or hire taxis to get ourselves and our dates where we wished to go. We went frequently to free outdoor band concerts on the grounds of the Capitol or the Lincoln Memorial. Another favorite social activity was the dances given frequently by the different government agencies.

Living in Washington immensely broadened my intellectual life as well as my social life. I repeatedly visited the city's many historic and fascinating buildings and museums. Among my favorites were the Library of Congress, the National Cathedral, and the Smithsonian Institution. I can recall my sensation of awe at gazing upon the actual Declaration of Independence in the Library of Congress, and upon Charles Lindbergh's plane, the *Spirit of St. Louis,* which was suspended from the ceiling of the Smithsonian. I also visited Mount Vernon, George Washington's home, where I stood in a mood of intense veneration before the tombs of the great founding father and his wife, Martha.

Simply being in the nation's capital was exciting. I went occasionally to the Capitol and sat in the visitors' gallery of the Senate chamber. There I heard discussions on the matters of the day, including the increasingly ominous words having to do with foreign affairs. I was not registered to vote in the presidential election of 1940, but I was an ardent admirer of President Franklin D. Roosevelt. I joined enthusiastically in the throng of admirers (one could almost say worshipers) that greeted him on the day of his inauguration for the third term. I also got a glimpse of him when he spoke on some occasion (probably Independence Day) in Arlington National Cemetery.

I lived in Washington for approximately fifteen months at this time. It was an exhilarating period of my life. I had no personal responsibilities other than those of my job; I had an income that was quite sufficient to my needs; I was healthy and happy; I was living the proverbial "life of Riley" in one of the most charming and interesting cities in the world. All of this would change in an instant.

The morning of Sunday, December 7, 1941, I ate a hearty breakfast and attended services at the Fourteenth Street Church of Christ. The news coming from the radio when I returned from church told of events that would forever change my life and that of the entire world.

Japanese forces had attacked the great American naval base at Pearl Harbor, Hawaii. This announcement was so incredible that we at first did not really believe it; we could not fully take it in. Everyone knew that Pearl Harbor was impregnable. All of us remembered the Orson Welles radio hoax about invaders from Mars; this must be a similar trick.

But no, all other radio programs now were dropped. The air was full of announcements and comments about Pearl Harbor. Before much time passed, we began to accept it; the Japanese really had attacked the famed base; they alone had not believed in its impregnability.

The following day all the Washington employees of the Department of the Interior, which included the National Park Service, were assembled in the large auditorium of the department's building to hear the broadcast of President Roosevelt's special message to Congress. The atmosphere was laden with grave anticipation. I dare say the empathy of listeners with a speaker has never been exceeded as he branded December 7 "a date which will live in infamy," called for a declaration of war against Japan, and intoned with majestic deliberation and solemnity, "We shall win the inevitable triumph, so help us God."

I had been registered for the military draft for more than a year, and almost immediately I received a letter ordering me to report for induction in mid-January 1942. I returned to my parents' home in Henderson in order to spend a few days with them and my friends before leaving for service and the unknown. I now attempted to enter the air corps for pilot training. Together with a lifelong Henderson friend, Earl Braden,

I went to a recruiting office in Jackson. He was accepted, I was not. To my keen disappointment, I was rejected because of a slight astigmatism in my left eye that prevented 20-20 vision. My military service would be that of a draftee.

Earl and I decided to bid Henderson a memorable farewell with a grand party. The affair went on for a full week. We went dancing with our dates and friends every night at the Y-Inn, a club on the highway outside of town. He and I were the hosts with the most. Because that part of Tennessee was "dry," we had commissioned a local pharmacist and friend to procure for us, on a buying trip to St. Louis, a case of Canadian Club whiskey. Neither of us could keep the alcohol at home, so the pharmacist kept it in the back section of his store along with the pharmaceuticals. We "set up" our friends throughout the duration of the week-long party. The beverage case was empty by the time we left town.

Becoming a Soldier

I did not object to going into the army; I welcomed it. The Japanese attack on our Pacific fleet, followed by Hitler's declaration of war against us, had ignited a conflagration of patriotic wrath among Americans. I fully shared this feeling, as did my parents. I was to report for service to the draft board in Alamo where I had been registered before leaving for Washington. My father would drive me to Alamo. Before daylight of the morning I was to report, I kissed my mother goodbye. She whispered through her tears, "Be a tough soldier." I could not reply, but nodded my head affirmatively.

The drive to Alamo with my father was, to say the least, an odd experience. He was a person of remarkable self-control; though he certainly harbored strong emotions, I had never seen him shed a tear. I could not remember ever being hugged or kissed by him, and I would have been inordinately embarrassed if he had done so at this time. On the way we chatted as casually as if we were on an outing. But when we shook hands and he said, "Goodbye, son," his voice broke. I stood mute, but I was stricken to the center, and now, after more than half a century, the moment comes back to me like an arrow in the heart.

The only ritual that occurred at the draft board headquarters was a brief health interrogation and physical examination, its primary purpose to determine whether anyone was showing symptoms of venereal disease. None were discovered. We then went by bus to Jackson, where we boarded a train bound for Chattanooga and an induction center at nearby Fort Oglethorpe, Georgia. There we were sworn into service, issued uniforms, given the Army General Classification Test (AGCT), a brief interview, and a more-or-less thorough physical examination. In answer to the examining medical officer's questions, I mentioned a few points in which I considered my health less than perfect. His comment to the soldier clerk who was trailing him with a pen and paper and clipboard was, "Husky." I felt a sense of pride in knowing I had passed the examination with flying colors.

One of my sharper memories of my brief stay at Fort Oglethorpe was the nightly scene in the post exchange, or canteen, where the inductees spent their evenings drinking Coke or beer and playing records on the jukebox. The favorite of these bewildered, homesick and lovesick boys, played repeatedly, was "Walking the Floor over You," a tune whose doleful lyrics set to a measured rhythm captured precisely the mood of the occasion: "I'm walking the floor over you, I can't sleep a wink it is true."

The AGCT was a combination intelligence and performance test. Despite being unable to solve many of the mathematics problems on it, I turned in a rather high score. The soldier who conducted my interview congratulated me on the results of the test and told me reassuringly that I would probably be assigned to some sort of personnel work. It seemed that army life was not to be particularly taxing after all.

The next morning the recruit assignments were posted on the barracks bulletin board. Could that possibly be my name listed under Infantry! There must be some mistake! No, no mistake. There it was: Private Charles P. Roland, Infantry Replacement Training Center, Camp Wheeler, Georgia. I was about to be initiated into an inimitable fraternity.

Camp Wheeler was located a few miles out of the city of Macon, in the red clay hills of rural Georgia. There we raw recruits were put through the rudiments of military training. The experience was absolutely new to me; I did not know how to salute or execute "right face." We went through the varied drills and tasks required to become a soldier, including road marches of as much as twenty-five miles a day, carrying heavy packs and rifles.

We were trained in the manual of arms and the care and operation of the army rifle. I was already a fair marksman because, like all southern boys and at least some southern girls, I had grown up shooting a .22 caliber rifle and a shotgun. But the heavy .30 caliber army rifle was a new experience. The first rifle issued to me was the 1903 model manually operated weapon of the kind that had been used by the United States Army in World War I. In fact, the pieces we received may very well have been handed down from that war.

Later we were issued Garand, or M-1, rifles. The Garand was a semi-automatic weapon: the bolt was operated by gas pressure from the exploding round of ammunition; the piece could be fired repeatedly, up to the eight rounds in the magazine, simply by pulling the trigger after each shot. The "kick" or recoil of the army rifle was considerable but not as great as that of my boyhood 12-gauge shotgun. I enjoyed firing at the targets on the 200-yard range.

I should be remiss in the telling of this story without giving a tribute to my platoon sergeant. He was a quintessential Georgia cracker, short in formal education but wiry and quick of body and mind. He had been a soldier since teenage, and he knew every trick of the trade.

His speech was direct and spectacularly pungent. Soon after we arrived at Camp Wheeler the company commander went through the squad rooms and inspected our footlockers. He found in them what he considered to be too many bottles of after-shave lotion and cologne; he ordered that all of it except one bottle of after-shave lotion and one deodorant be disposed of. The sergeant conveyed this order at the evening Retreat formation, introducing it with the announcement, "A soldier don't suppose to smell like no whore. He just suppose to smell like a clean man." Whether in fact we smelled like clean men is open to question; doubtless, in the sergeant's mind, we ceased to smell like whores.

My favorite from the sergeant was his explanation of a certain type of fire known as enfilade fire. The field manual definition was pretty heavy. It went something like this: "Enfilade fire is that in which the long axis of the beaten zone falls along the long axis of the target." The sergeant quoted the definition with an exaggerated preciseness; then, bringing a rifle to his shoulder, he sighted it at an imaginary target to his extreme left, and explained: "It's like you're firin' down a line of Krauts or Japs sittin' like blackbirds shittin' maulberries along a bob-war fence." His definition was as colorful as it was functional; nobody ever forgot it.

When the training cycle ended I was kept at Camp Wheeler as a temporary member of the cadre to help train a company of fresh draftees. I began to feel more like a soldier, especially after I was designated an "acting" PFC (private first class) and entitled to wear a stripe on my sleeve, even though the stripe was nothing more than a piece of white adhesive tape with my acting rank printed on it.

Soon another opportunity arose. An announcement from on high appeared on the company bulletin board saying the army seriously needed 75,000 additional second lieutenants. All soldiers who had received a score of as much as 110 on the classification test were urged to apply for Officer Candidate School (OCS). I was qualified to apply.

I turned this over carefully in my mind. If accepted into OCS, could I pass the course? It would be demanding both mentally and physically. Did I really wish to be an officer? It would bring me more pay, higher prestige, and a more attractive uniform, but I would be taking on a load of responsibility. Also, the prevailing army wisdom said, "Never volunteer for anything; be as inconspicuous as possible." Finally, I was pretty sure I knew why the army so keenly needed so many new second lieutenants: they were the most expendable, suffered the highest casualty rate, of any group of soldiers.

In the end I decided to try for it. I was accepted and I passed the physical examination, which was decidedly more thorough than the one I had been given at the induction center. Next I passed a rigorous interview by a board of officers. Then I was sent to a one-month OCS preparatory school at Camp Wheeler. It provided excellent training; it was actually an abbreviated OCS course; the officers and noncommissioned officers conducting it made it as rigorous as possible. I passed the course and received orders to proceed to Fort Benning, Georgia, for OCS.

The OCS course lasted three months, from mid-July to mid-October—in other words, through the hottest season of the South. The training was grueling, but any other type would have been worse than useless, it would have been criminal; we were being prepared to command young Americans in mortal combat.

Taxing as the experience was, it was one of the most exhilarating periods of my life. OCS was probably as near as possible to being a true meritocracy. There were no formal educational requirements for eligibility. My class of more than two hundred contained a few college graduates, including me, and a larger number of soldiers who had completed some college work but not enough for a degree. I am of the impression that the great majority of my OCS classmates had no college education; probably some had not finished high school. At least in theory, all of us were there because we had demonstrated we had the stuff to be there.

The intellectual demands of the course were not difficult for me. I ended up doing a bit of informal tutoring in map and compass reading and small-unit tactics to some of the other candidates in my squad room. The physical demands were tough, but my former athletic experience now stood me in good stead. I found that I could run the obstacle course regularly in the top third of my class, occasionally in the top tenth, and once I came in second. The hardest job I did in OCS was that of serving as a crew member in an 81-millimeter mortar exercise that required us to advance from one position to another, moving a few hundred yards each time. The temperature that day was in the neighborhood of 100 degrees. The crew rotated tasks in carrying the mortar tube, bipod, and baseplate, each, as I recall, weighing about seventy-five pounds. I decided that was a hard way to make a living.

I passed the OCS course and received my commission as a second lieutenant, a "shavetail" or "ninety-day wonder," to use the army parlance. To my surprise and gratification, the entire class was placed on an order granting us a few days of leave and assigning us to the same division, the 99th Infantry Division. The unit was located, or would be when it was formed, at Camp Van Dorn, Mississippi, just outside the town of Centreville. We arrived there on or about the same day from all over the nation. I was assigned to the 3rd Battalion of the 394th Infantry Regiment.

The place looked decidedly inhospitable. Centreville was a more or less typical small town of the Deep South of that era. Growing cotton had traditionally been the major enterprise of the surrounding countryside. The Great Depression had pretty much killed the cotton economy; the area was full of abandoned farms, dotted with farmhouses whose roofs were caving in, and with small family cemeteries grown up in weeds that stood ten to fifteen feet tall. The forlorn looks on the faces of the recently drafted boys from such cities as Pittsburgh and

Cleveland, standing at trainside in their ill-fitting and sagging uniforms, with their barracks bags stuffed with extra clothing on their shoulders, told the story. They believed they had died and gone to hell.

They were wrong on the first part; they had not died. But many of them soon became convinced that they were rather close on the second part: that Camp Van Dorn and Centreville were at least a reasonable facsimile of hell. One of the young lieutenants of my battalion returned to camp from town with the excited and horrific pronouncement that everyone there was in an advanced stage of tuberculosis. How did he know this? From the splotches of dried blood he had seen all over the sidewalk! I educated him on the Rorschach images left by chewing tobacco.

The camp was unfinished, construction in progress. Even when the construction was completed, the place was almost uninhabitable. The barracks were one-story buildings of coarse raw lumber covered over with sheets of black roofing paper. They were heated with potbellied, coal-fired heaters that stood in the aisles between the rows of cots. Soldiers occupying cots near them roasted; those whose cots were farther away froze.

Winters in that part of the world are mild by Minnesota or North Dakota standards, but they are not warm. From mid-December to mid-March the thermometer is likely to drop into the twenties any night, and the atmosphere is abnormally humid. The great majority of our troops promptly developed severe respiratory infections; never before or since have I heard such a barrage of coughing and wheezing. The makeshift hospitals were overwhelmed with the sick. Fortunately, we suffered no deadly epidemic of influenza or pneumonia. Within a few weeks the soldiers were well and hearty.

They were, in fact, probably more healthy than they had ever been, because of the nutritious quality of their food and the almost constant physical exercise required of them in the form of calisthenics, running obstacle courses, and marching. We tried conscientiously to teach them everything we had learned about soldiering. Many of the boys from the cities had never fired a weapon; they were both excited and alarmed by the experience. Just as I had been transformed from a civilian into a citizen soldier a few months earlier, they were now transformed likewise.

I served as a platoon leader, then as the battalion S-3, the staff officer in charge of training while in garrison.

The proximity of the city of Natchez (about forty miles) made life at Camp Van Dorn bearable for me. Set on a high bluff on the east bank of the Mississippi River, resplendent with live oaks, magnolias, and a profusion of flowers, the town was the site of a remarkable cluster of stately antebellum mansions. Many army wives, in order to be near their husbands, rented rooms in the great houses. Lt. Charles Allen's wife (he was my roommate at camp) had a room on the second floor of Stanton Hall, the largest of the mansions. On numerous occasions my date and I enjoyed refreshments with the Allens on their balcony an arm's length from the tips of the branches of one of the spectacular live oaks that stood on the grounds. The citizens of the town, including especially the young women, were gracious and hospitable. I spent every weekend there when I was not on duty. The city's Eola Hotel became something of my home away from home. I can never forget Natchez.

The in-garrison training ended in midsummer of 1943. Then, for a month, we engaged in what we called "little maneuvers." These exercises occurred in the outlying areas of the Camp Van Dorn reservation. They involved mock battles between a part of the division and the rest of it, say, two of the three regiments attacking the third regiment. We lived in the field, without benefit of shelter, beds, or bathing facilities.

The heat was almost unbearable, the sweat and grime incredible. We emitted a collective aroma that probably could be detected long before we could be seen. Our drinking water was pumped out of the area creeks, filtered, and chlorinated. It was distributed in large canvas bags (Lister bags) from which we filled our canteens. According to army doctrine, the water in the bags was cooled by a process of gradual evaporation through the canvas. Big joke! It was as warm as the creeks themselves; in addition, it bore the distinctive taste of rotting leaves.

Following the little maneuvers in Mississippi came the "big maneuvers" in Louisiana. These exercises involved far larger numbers of troops: entire divisions in mock battle against other divisions. This went on from mid-September until a few days before Christmas of 1943. In my judgment, these exercises were excellent training for combat. We became far more hardened through marching and living out of doors. The last three or four weeks were cold enough at night to put a film of ice on the puddles of water. Fatigue and familiarity had made us largely indifferent to the threat of the wildlife of the area; in addition to the myriad of mosquitoes and ticks, Louisiana was host to all four species of the continent's venomous snakes, including water moccasins, rattlesnakes, copperheads, and corals. Just for good measure, there were also lots of sting-tailed scorpions.

I once read that the German army made its maneuvers so hard that the soldiers welcomed being sent into combat. I cannot say this was generally true of our maneuvers, but I recall one episode in them that matched anything in combat in its demands on our physical stamina. This was a cross-country march of thirty-eight miles completed in twenty-three hours late in the course of the exercises. We did much of it along trails in the woods, fording creeks and climbing their embankments. The final six hours occurred between midnight and dawn in a torrential rainfall.

That exercise brought me near the absolute limit of my endurance. Toward the end I stumbled along in something of a trance of fatigue and began to hallucinate mildly, seeing in front of me what appeared to be houses cozy with fires burning on the hearths, but which turned into pine trees when I came abreast of them. Once when I told another soldier about this experience he matched my story with one of his own. He said he had previously been a cook's helper in the company kitchen and that late in the march he began to see ahead of him what seemed to be giant stacks of hotcakes with smoke curling temptingly upward to the sky. Alas, they too were transformed into pine trees when he reached them.

The final exercise involved an attack across the Sabine River, which separates Louisiana from Texas. For a week we had been living in an icy drizzle of rain. We believed we were as miserable as a human ever gets to be. We crossed the river in rubber boats before dawn, jumped out in water up to our waists, and slogged through the ankle-deep mud to form a small defensive perimeter that was to be expanded into a full bridgehead.

A memorable humorous incident took place on the Texas bank of the Sabine. For some time I had carried on a friendly banter with a young lieutenant from Texas over the relative merits of our natal states. When we reached the Texas bank of the stream, he walked up to me, threw himself face down, and ostentatiously kissed the mud that reeked of oil and God only knows what else. I conceded his superior devotion to his state.

By the time the Louisiana maneuvers ended, except for an occasional night in a nearby town during a break between exercises, I had not slept on a bed or within walls for approximately four months; unbelievable as it sounds, I had become so accustomed to sleeping on the ground that beds for a while actually felt somewhat uncomfortable to me. The maneuvers gave us invaluable logistical training, practice in the movement and supply of large bodies of troops in the field.

I did get into the town of Natchitoches, which lay on the eastern edge of the maneuver area, two or three times. I retain vivid memories of parties in the Hotel Nakatosh (a phonetic spelling of the town name), raucous affairs featuring ample quantities of alcohol and loud talk and laughter. There was no room service for drinks. We carried our own bottles, bought a twenty-five-pound block of ice at the local ice plant, chipped it up with a trench knife, and in the absence of an ice bucket in the room, kept it in the well-scrubbed (I hope!) wash basin of the bathroom.

By an intriguing coincidence, my future wife was then a student at the state college in Natchitoches. We were prevented from becoming acquainted at the time by the suspicions of the school's dean of women. So suspicious and protective was she that she campused her wards on those occasions when we came into town.

We were under the impression that we would be sent overseas as soon as the maneuvers ended. Instead, we were sent to Camp Maxey, Texas, near the town of Paris in the northeastern part of the state, a few miles south of the Oklahoma border. Camp Maxey seemed almost like paradise to us. The barracks were traditional two-story buildings far superior to those at Camp Van Dorn; they were heated by furnaces and steam radiators. Paris was a much more attractive town than Centreville. But, ironically, after enduring the rigors of maneuvers without a sniffle, in the relative luxury of my new surroundings I promptly came down with a respiratory infection so severe that I had to be hospitalized. Not until after about ten days did I return to duty. Hardly was I again on my feet when I was ordered back to Fort Benning for an advanced course of training that lasted several weeks. Its major emphasis was on battalion logistics and tactics; I was now a captain, and the training would be invaluable to me in the near future.

Compared with OCS, this tour at Fort Benning was decidedly pleasant. My companions and I made it more so by frequent weekend trips to Atlanta, which was one of the country's favorite visitation sites for soldiers. I made most of these trips in company with Lt. Wesley Zuber, the communications officer of my battalion, who was back at Fort Benning in an advanced communications course at the time.

The history of the division now underwent a sharp turn as the result of larger events. Casualties among infantrymen had been far heavier than anticipated in the Pacific, North Africa, and Italy. Replacements had to be found for these losses. The authorities turned to all noncombat units and to the infantry divisions that were still in the United States. In early 1944 they took about half of the soldiers out of our line companies and sent them overseas to the depleted divisions there. Soon they replenished us with troops drawn mainly from the Army Specialized Training Program (ASTP). This was an operation in which soldiers selected for their outstanding intelligence and education were sent back to college after finishing basic army training.

When I returned to Camp Maxey in the early spring I found that I had been assigned as the company commander of Company I, 3rd Battalion, 394th Infantry. I found also that something like half of the company troops were new replacements, most of them former ASTP men just off the nation's campuses. The immediate mission of the entire division was to assimilate these replacements into the unit, bring them up to standard in their training, and carry the entire unit through tactical exercises designed to remedy any deficiencies noted by the umpires (observers who rated our performance) during maneuvers.

I soon discovered that the ASTP replacements, though deficient in training, were exceptionally quick to learn. They eventually would become superb soldiers. Their only training shortage in the end was that of the toughening experience of maneuvers. We trained hard throughout the summer, firing all kinds of infantry weapons on the ranges and carrying out a great variety of small-unit tactical exercises. We also performed a few exercises of battalion strength with artillery support.

In these exercises we employed live ammunition, which obviously added elements of realism and danger. On one occasion I was frightened almost out of my wits when I discovered I had advanced some of my soldiers farther than they were supposed to be when the artillery rounds began exploding a few yards ahead of them. Fortunately, nobody was hurt in this incident. But on another occasion a battalion soldier not in my company was killed by a ricocheting bullet during a practice attack on a mock town.

We also ran an obstacle course that involved crawling through barbed-wire entanglements under live machine-gun fire. The hiss of bullets streaking inches above the back develops an extraordinary skill in flattening out and hugging the ground. All of these activities were non-subtle reminders that real combat was not far in our future.

I fully expected to serve in combat as the commander of Company I. This is what I wished to do. There was a saying in the army that the job of company commander was the best of all the jobs in the service; it brought the commander and the troops closer together than any other assignment. I had a strong sense of responsibility and pride for the men in my company; I did everything in my power to train them well for the ordeal that lay ahead.

I was not destined to lead the company in combat. We had a new and inexperienced battalion commander who felt overwhelmed by the job of training all of the new arrivals. I was told by a friend that when the battalion commander was singing the blues one night in the regimental officers' club, the regimental S-3 said to him, "Why don't you bring Captain Roland up to your staff as the battalion S-3 and turn the training job over to him? He was a teacher in civilian life and he has already had experience in the duties of the S-3." In midsummer I suddenly found myself in that position again. The assignment was difficult; I did my best to carry it out effectively.

One of the most unexpected tasks that befell me and my fellow officers had nothing to do with soldiering as such. Aware that we soon would be crossing one ocean or another, the military authorities issued an order that all personnel be tested for aquatic proficiency and those who could not swim be taught to do so. The testing and teaching were carried out in a lake on the Camp Maxey reservation. To my amazement, more than half of the soldiers failed the test. The success of the program is open to question; I seriously doubt that anyone who could not already swim was taught to do so well enough to do him any good in an emergency. Fortunately, we were spared such an emergency.

As we approached the end of our training, only five of us officers remained who had been in the battalion throughout its history. All had begun our careers at Camp Van Dorn as new second lieutenants. Besides me, there was Capt. Joseph Shank of Toledo, Ohio, 1st Lt. Charles Allen of St. Louis, Missouri, 1st Lt. Neil Brown of Lincoln, Nebraska, and 1st Lt. Wesley Zuber of Pensacola, Florida. We had become warm personal friends, and we comprised the major element of continuity in the battalion. I believe this provided it a strong measure of unit cohesion, one of the qualities deemed to be vitally important to combat effectiveness.

In mid-August we received the orders we had been expecting; the division was placed on alert for overseas movement. The camp became electric with anticipation. At first we did not know our destination. I crossed my fingers and silently prayed it would be Europe instead of the reeking jungles of the South Pacific. I did not have long to wait; soon came an order placing me (because of my assignment as S-3) on the division advance party. We were to proceed by commercial rail transportation to the New York City port of embarkation. My prayer had been answered; we were bound for Europe.

The trip of the advance party to New York was itself exciting. The train was a regular civilian train, but we enjoyed first-class sleeping and dining accommodations. Our orders required us to remove all unit insignia from our uniforms and maintain silence as to our destination. In keeping with our rather mysterious demeanor and the somber and determined mood of the nation at the time, our civilian fellow passengers seemed to regard us with an awe that kept them at arm's length.

We detrained at Fort Hamilton on Long Island. To our unrestrained joy, we remained there for some three weeks. After a brief period of sailing instructions we had no duties and were free to go into downtown Manhattan every day. We had only to be present for the reveille formation each morning to receive whatever orders and instructions awaited us. Accordingly, we spent most of the time in the big city.

It was humming. By late afternoon every day, the lobbies of the great hotels were literally jammed with young women seeking escorts. We were willing subjects. We dined in the best restaurants and danced to the music of the renowned big bands: my favorite at the moment was

Sammy Kaye's orchestra emitting its smooth and lilting rhythms out into the glittering ballroom on the top floor of one of the skyscraper hotels.

The brief interlude in New York City was immeasurably supercharged in our emotions by the keen awareness that it was indeed a brief interlude; that it could and would end in the twinkling of an eye and we would be on our way into the toils of war. This was brought home to me in a very personal way. About two weeks after my arrival at Fort Hamilton I was informed in a telephone conversation with my mother that a lifelong friend of mine from Henderson, Joe Rainey, also a soldier, was at the New York port of embarkation, and that his wife, Jasper, also a lifelong friend, was in the city to bid him goodbye before he shipped out.

My mother gave me Jasper's hotel number. I telephoned her at once and arranged to have dinner with her that evening. She had been in New York a day or two without being able to get in touch with her husband. We dined together and reminisced fondly about our early years in Henderson. I promised to try to find her husband; we arranged to have dinner together again the following evening. It did not occur. The next morning at reveille my comrades and I were informed that our unit was on alert for departure and that all communications with the outside had been severed. I did not see either Jasper or Joe until we were together in Henderson well over a year later. Then I learned that the two of them had made no contact in New York. Jasper was my last touch with my native heath prior to embarkation.

Two days later we moved to the port by truck convoy. I could not believe the manner in which this took place. After all the warnings about the need for secrecy, we rode slowly that bright fall morning through the streets of Manhattan. We were in full combat arms and gear; the sidewalks and windows were thronged with waving, cheering, weeping spectators, many of the women throwing kisses with both hands. Except for the absence of a military band playing the rousing World War I song "Over There," it could have been a Hollywood spectacular representation of troops leaving for an overseas war.

Into the Line

An astonishing and delightful surprise awaited us at the wharf. I marveled at the size of the ship tied up there. Could it be one of the fabled British liners, *Queen Mary* or *Queen Elizabeth*? Yes, though the name was painted out, we learned soon after boarding that we were indeed on the *Queen Mary*. Unlike the unfortunate soldiers in the main body of the division, who would be crossing the Atlantic on ordinary troop ships, we of the advance party would cross in high style.

We soon found that our style was a tad lower than we had initially thought it would be. As officers we were jammed some twelve or more into a stateroom designed for two persons; we slept in bunks that were stacked a few inches apart all the way to the ceiling. We bathed and shaved in salty seawater because the ship's water tanks would accommodate only enough fresh water for drinking and cooking. Still, compared with the enlisted men who were packed into the dark and smelly hold of the vessel, we were in clover. We dined in the regular dining room, with white linen tablecloths and napkins, and we were served by regular British waiters.

Hardly were we settled on the *Queen Mary* when we received another tremendous surprise. We learned that among our fellow passengers was one of the two or three most famous and important men in the world. Prime Minister Winston Churchill of Great Britain, fresh from his recent Quebec conference with President Roosevelt, was returning to England on our ship. I was overwhelmed, for I held the most unrestrained admiration for Churchill.

According to our briefing aboard ship, she and her sister queen sailed without escort. They were said to be too swift for a submarine to get in position to torpedo them. At first I was a bit dubious about this information, but when I learned Churchill was a passenger my doubts vanished. The trip had to be safe; certainly, the authorities would take no risks on him. Imagine my emotions years later upon reading in the published diary of his physician, Lord Moran, that the presumably imperturbable prime minister himself was very much concerned over the possibility of the ship's being hit. Obviously my presence aboard did not reassure him as his presence reassured me.

Churchill and his party occupied a restricted section of the ship and I did not get a glance of him until near the end of the voyage when he came down and gave a brief talk in the grand ballroom. He spoke of the marvelous cooperation between our two kindred nations in the prodigious struggle against Hitler. He received a giant ovation.

The trip across the ocean was uneventful. The water was relatively calm, and the great ship plowed along smoothly. The food and music were good. There were a number of general hospital parties aboard; the nurses were pleasant company. We lolled on blankets spread on the upper deck next to the huge stacks, which provided warmth against the sharp atmosphere of the north Atlantic. The war seemed far away.

We landed during the night at Grennock, Scotland, boarded a train that was standing on the pier, rode all night and much of the next day, and stopped on a pier at Southampton where a black and sinister-looking ship stood waiting. Suddenly the war seemed much nearer than it had while we were on the *Queen Mary*. I had been almost deliriously excited and anxious to set foot on the soil of England. Instead, I had traveled some three-fourths of the length of Great Britain without once touching land.

One hilarious incident of the trip to Southampton left its mark. When our train was standing temporarily in the large railyard of a city whose name I do not recall, the children of the neighborhood, which was unmistakably slummy, swarmed like alley cats over the high board fences enclosing the yard and lined up along the track begging for handouts. Soldiers tossed them candy, cookies, and coins. One enterprising GI flipped out a package of C-ration crackers. These crackers were virtually inedible; we speculated that they were hardtack held over from the Civil War.

The package landed at the feet of a little girl of perhaps eight. She was roughly clad, but she had long braids down her back, and her face was thin but pretty. She made no move to retrieve the crackers. Instead, she cast a single disdainful glance at them, looked up with a perceptible sneer on her countenance, and said in that unforgettable English brogue, "Those fookin' biscuits are useless." A roar of assent went up from all within hearing and was echoed from car to car down the length of the train. From that moment, the expression became standard in the regiment for anything deemed worthless. The little girl who coined it received a shower of goodies. She probably had rehearsed the act many times.

We crossed the channel without mishap and landed at Omaha Beach, which had been the scene of savage fighting and heavy bloodshed some three months earlier. We pitched tents and encamped a short distance back from the beach to await the arrival of the main body of the division, which was scheduled to land at the port of Cherbourg. We were in our location for several days and had an opportunity to wander about and survey the ruins of the villages that had come under bombardment during the great invasion.

Then we received word that we were to return to England. The Cherbourg port had been so wrecked by the Germans that the landing of our troops there would be impossible; they had been diverted to England. Back across the Channel we went on an LST (Landing Ship, Tank) to rejoin the main body of the division in southern England. My battalion was located just outside the village of Beaminster, which is in Dorsetshire four or five miles from the town of Dorchester. At last I got an opportunity to see a bit of England.

I was enthralled by the beauty and what I considered the quaintness of England. Immediately adjacent to our encampment was a lovely park of several acres filled with green grass and stately trees; deer grazed and wandered throughout it. I had the feeling that I was in a fairyland, like Dorothy in the Land of Oz.

My initial contact with the English people occurred my first evening in England when a group of us walked into Dorchester in search of excitement. We soon found it in the presence of a group of teenage girls who greeted us with a most cordial "'Ello there, Yanks." To our question as to where the fun occurred in Dorchester, they replied, "We'll show you. Come with us." We did, and they led us to the local pub. On the way, they demonstrated their spirit and energy by grasping what I took to be a hitching rail in front of one of the town shops and "skinning the cat" on it, billowing out their skirts and flashing their underpants in our amazed faces as they turned their somersaults.

The pub itself provided me a new and interesting experience. It was jammed with friendly people. Standing at the bar, foot on brass rail, and quaffing the warm, dark ale of the place, was a group of sturdy young women in uniform. I approached one of them and inquired their identity. "We're land army," I was told. "What do you do?" I asked. "We fell trees and load them on lorries [British for trucks]," she replied with a flex of the considerable muscles of her arms and shoulders. "'Ave an ile [translated, 'Have an ale'], Yank." I did.

From the pub we went to a fish-and-chips shop, where I enjoyed the experience of eating fried fish and what I had always heard called French-fried potatoes. The manner in which the food was served intrigued me: a portion of fish atop the chips in a cone made from a rolled-up newspaper. We salted the fish and chips and sprinkled them with vinegar from a bottle with a perforated cap. This fare was delicious to all of us because for many days we had been eating nothing but C-rations, canned emergency rations consisting of meat and beans.

We remained in England for two or three weeks awaiting the shipment of the entire division to the mainland. We spent this interval training by map and blackboard tactical exercises, practicing the disassembling and reassembling of weapons, and seeing to the maintenance of vehicles and other equipment. We kept in physical shape by performing vigorous calisthenics and making rapid daily marches of five miles out and back.

One of the marches provided a diverting incident. We had stopped for a ten-minute break at the end of the outgoing five miles. A pretty young woman came pedaling her bike up the hill, her white thighs exposed as gusts of wind whipped up her skirt. The soldiers grinned and offered audible comments. She stopped her bike when she got to me and asked in obvious indignation, "I say, Captain, 'aven't those blokes of yours ever seen a woman before?" I was tempted to say, "Not so much of one recently as just now," but I held my tongue, and she rode on.

Soon we received orders placing us on a twenty-four-hour alert and restricting us to our unit areas. Nothing happened for two or three days, and our battalion commander decided to stage a party. We arranged for musicians and invited a group of nurses from a nearby military hospital. I was dancing with an attractive young woman from Pennsylvania and flattering myself that I was making progress with her when she stopped me with the information that she was married and her husband was fighting in an infantry division on the Continent.

Just as I was digesting this piece of information, a courier arrived from regimental headquarters with a message that ended the party abruptly. The division was ordered to the Continent immediately; our battalion's organic transportation (the company kitchen trucks, the antitank guns and their tow vehicles, and a dozen or more jeeps, many of them loaded with machine guns and mortars) was to move out early the following morning for the port of embarkation at Southampton. The battalion executive officer, Maj. George Clayton, assigned me the task of commanding the convoy to the port. I spent most of the rest of the night issuing instructions for the drivers and crews of the vehicles and checking to see that everything was in order for the move. We pulled out at 0600 and reached our destination that morning. The war, which until now had been something of an abstraction, something happening to other people, suddenly began to seem terribly personal.

We spent the night in a huge warehouse that had been converted into a barracks. After the lights were out and all of us on our cots, the lights came back on and an officer appeared with a bundle of papers. He announced that we were to be given an opportunity to vote by paper ballot in the presidential election. I then cast my first political ballot: for Franklin D. Roosevelt to serve an unprecedented fourth term as president of the United States.

We boarded an LST the following day and set out across the English Channel. I was pretty cocky about my seamanship; I had now crossed the Atlantic once and the Channel twice without a hint of seasickness. I was confident that I was immune to that malady. How mistaken I was! This time the weather became stormy, the water unruly; our shallow-draft vessel pitched and yawed like an unbroken mustang. I thought I would die of seasickness before we reached land. And I thought we would never reach land—the voyage took almost as long as the passage of the Atlantic on the *Queen Mary*.

The most memorable event of the crossing was a Sunday-morning worship service the first day out. It was conducted by my battalion chaplain, 1st Lt. Edwin Hampton, down in the ship's tank hold. The altar from which he spoke and served the elements of Communion rested on the hood of a jeep. The soldier audience sat in vehicles or half-sat leaning against the barrels of the cannons, which stood like silent, menacing beasts awaiting their prey. The service was punctuated by the snapping and groaning of the chains and turnbuckles that held the vehicles and guns in place against the rolling motions of the ship.

The chaplain spoke briefly and quietly, but with deep emotion, of the mighty crusade on which we were engaged. He called it a worthy cause, blessed by heaven. Then, elevating his right hand in a gesture of beatitude, he said, "The Lord be with you and keep you. The Lord give you strength in the day of battle." I was especially close to Chaplain Hampton because he was a minister of the Church of Christ, the religious body in which I had grown up and of which I was a member. How could any of us anticipate that this kind man of faith would be among the first to die!

We landed at Le Havre, France, at midnight amid an icy drizzle of rain. I shuffled down the ramp, still dizzy from seasickness and as weak as a kitten from loss of food. A flashlight beam struck my eyes and an authoritative voice came out of the darkness: "Captain, give your name, assignment, and organization." I recognized the voice of my division commander and gave him the demanded information. "You are hereby placed in command of troop convoy Blue Five," he said. "My aide will escort you to the convoy. You are to conduct it to the town of Aubel, Belgium, as expeditiously as possible. He will provide you with the necessary maps and information. Any questions?" "No questions, sir," I replied with a note of self-confidence that I definitely did not feel.

The aide and I walked to a waiting jeep and climbed aboard. Seldom since becoming an officer did I ever wish to exchange places with an enlisted man. Now, bouncing over the cobblestones in this exotic place so far from home, I felt terribly lost and inadequate. I experienced a pang of envy for the soldiers who sat in the trucks, wrapped like mummies in their blankets and tenting, sleeping like infants who had just been fed and burped. The convoy contained twenty trucks loaded with thirty soldiers each and their arms and equipment.

For three days and two nights we rode, stopping only for occasional relief and refueling intervals. The route was supposed to be indicated by markers, but occasionally the signs were missing and I would become lost. When this happened, I stopped the convoy until I made a reconnaissance and found the route again. Once I was obliged to roam across the entire breadth of a large, blacked-out city in the night.

Our fixed procedure called for the motor officer, who ordinarily rode at the tail of the column, to come to the head of it when we stopped. When I had found the route and returned to the convoy he would proceed back to the tail of the column, stopping at each truck to wake up the driver. Meanwhile, I would wait a prescribed amount of time before moving out in order to allow him to carry out his assignment and get back to his tail position. But on the occasion when I had to traverse the entire city, our procedure failed because a driver in the middle of the convey fell asleep again after he had been awakened, leaving the rear half of the column standing while I moved out with the front half. Miles down the road the motor officer came racing to catch me and inform me what had happened. I then waited until he could return and bring up the other trucks. The whole experience was extremely upsetting.

We arrived at our destination in the late afternoon of November 11, amid an eight-inch snowfall. I was exhausted beyond words, my eyes so inflamed from grime and loss of sleep that a bead of pus stood in the inner corner of each. The troops spent the night in tents pitched in an open field between the villages of Aubel and Henri Chapelle. I was fortunate enough to spend the night in a farmhouse with a few of my fellow officers and a cluster of Belgian girls who were interested in talking about an American crooner they called "Beeng Crows-bee" and an American city they called "Sheek-ago."

I wished to be sociable; the spirit was willing but the flesh was lamentably weak. After a hot meal, some eyedrops and APC tablets (reinforced aspirin) administered by the battalion surgeon, and a long swig of sacramental wine mercifully supplied by the battalion chaplain, I fell into a profound sleep and did not stir for eighteen hours, when I was awakened to receive fresh orders from my battalion commander.

The regiment had been ordered to move directly into the line; I was to join a regimental advance party right away. Our mission was to reconnoiter the routes up to a location just behind the line, establish unit assembly areas there, and guide the units into these areas. We spent that night in a shell-damaged house in a village named Murringen, within sound of gunfire from the front. I slept only intermittently and had lots of time to meditate.

The next day the division took position in the line. The setting, in the Ardennes region of Belgium, was an area of rugged hills and steep ravines covered with fir forests interspersed among open pastureland. It was a favorite vacation resort spot for the Belgian population. My battalion line lay in a forest where the cone-shaped evergreens standing in deep snow and sparkling with crystals created a beautiful scene that could have been the model for a Hallmark Christmas card. Within the battalion area stood an abandoned tavern bearing the name "Chalet Buffalo Bill."

We had been placed here because it was a quiet sector of the Allied line and deemed an ideal location for a green division to get a feeling for the front without being heavily engaged. The bulk of the Allied forces were concentrated north and south of us, awaiting the return of spring, when a great offensive would be launched to end the war in the west. The terrain of the Ardennes was considered unsuited to large-scale offensive action by either army.

We felt reasonably comfortable in our position and also reasonably safe, though we did suffer a few casualties from enemy fire and antipersonnel mines. My close friend Lt. Charlie Allen was killed here leading a reconnaissance patrol. He was the division's first fatal casualty.

His death caused me to draw closer to my other friends who were original members of the battalion. The day Allen was killed the company commander of Company L was also killed, and Lieutenant Brown became the commander of the company. A few days later he was promoted to the rank of captain. I visited him to congratulate him and found him still wearing the single bar of a lieutenant. When I asked him why, he said he had no captain's bars. Since I had an extra set, I pulled off the ones I was wearing and pinned them on his collar. Forty years later, while visiting my wife and me in Lexington, Kentucky, he returned the bars to me.

In moving into the Ardennes line we were informed by higher headquarters that we faced only a handful of defeated and demoralized German troops, and that they were supported by only two batteries of horse-drawn artillery. An enormous surprise awaited us.

What the division actually faced was an immense enemy force assembled by Hitler a few miles behind their line. Its mission was that of attacking the Allied armies and aborting their offensive against the German homeland. Our authorities were blissfully unaware of what was about to occur. I have called this the "Shiloh syndrome" because of its similarity to the situation and thinking of Gen. U. S. Grant on the eve of the great Civil War battle of Shiloh, in which he was taken by complete surprise.

Our division of some 13,000 men held a front of about twenty-two miles, so thinly manned that it was hardly more than an outpost line. To give some idea of how thin this was in a functional sense, I would point out that the Union army of about 95,000 in the battle of Gettysburg held a front of approximately five miles. Vastly aggravating our situation, our right flank was seriously exposed; a gap of several thousand yards lay between us and the next division in line.

Hugh Cole, in his authoritative history of the Ardennes campaign, opens his narrative with a description of the disposition of the opposing armies on the eve of the fighting. He points out that the main effort of the Germans was to be delivered by the Sixth Panzer Army against the attenuated line of the 99th Infantry Division. He comes to my unit, the 394th Infantry Regiment, last. Here is what he says: "The fateful position of the 394th would bring against it the main effort of the I SS Panzer Corps and, indeed, that of the Sixth Panzer Army."

A thunderclap of German artillery fire struck us at dawn of December 16. When it lifted we found ourselves under vicious assault by enemy infantry and tanks. All that day and the next we fought desperately for survival. Throughout the entire period I wandered in a daze, a nightmare that I kept hoping I would soon awaken from. An enemy tank stopped by our fire at a thousand yards resembled a child's toy until my binoculars showed the bodies of the crewmen hanging like rag dolls out of the smoking turret hatch. A young lieutenant danced rubber-legged until he twisted slowly and revealed a blue bullet hole in the middle of his forehead. Chaplain Hampton and his assistant lay headless beside their disabled jeep, cleanly decapitated by an exploding enemy shell. Our entire regiment seemed in peril of destruction.

During the night of the 16th a powerful enemy panzer column bypassed our right flank through the open gap in the line and struck deep behind us. By noon of the 17th the village of Losheimergraben, which stood at a vital crossroads at the center of the regimental line, was a shambles of blasted and burning houses and vehicles and was littered with the dead of both sides. We had lost all unit organization above the company level; our defense was chiefly that of small units fighting independently for survival.

During the morning of the 17th I visited Captain Brown in his company's isolated position at the Losheimergraben railway station, just outside the town. The company had repelled a dangerous enemy attack the previous day. Brown was my closest army friend now that Charlie Allen was dead, and I had great confidence in his character and judgment. For a time we discussed the grimness of the situation, then, as I was preparing to return to the battalion command post, he said, "Charlie, get the hell out of here while you can." This sounded like good advice and I complied at once. As I left I wondered whether I would ever see him again.

In the early afternoon we received orders to be prepared to withdraw from the overextended and vulnerable position. My battalion commander, Maj. Norman More, sent me to obtain information from the 1st Battalion commander as to his plans of withdrawal so that the movements would be coordinated. When I reached him he said he had formed no plan and could not do so until he had surveyed his battalion line, which he was just setting out to do. He told me to accompany him on his survey.

Besides the battalion commander and me, our party consisted of a radio operator with a heavy radio on his back and two or three riflemen for protection. We approached the village of Losheimergraben, where continuous firing went on, then veered to the left into woods where we wandered for the remainder of the afternoon. The battalion commander repeatedly attempted to make radio contact with his companies but so far as I could determine was never able to do so. I was later told that for security purposes the radio signals had been changed that afternoon. I had the feeling that we were completely lost.

At last, late in the afternoon, we came upon the executive officer of the 2nd Battalion, Maj. Benjamin Legare of Charleston. He was a diminutive man physically but an exceptionally bright and dedicated officer. He was once described to me as being composed of nothing but brains. He and I had crossed the ocean together on the *Queen Mary;* we were very close friends.

Legare was standing by his jeep in a small clearing in the woods. He told us that the entire regiment had been ordered to withdraw to the town of Murringen, five or six miles behind us; that all of his battalion except a thin rear guard had gone; that the rear guard was now pulling out and the enemy would be upon us at any moment. He had been ordered to report to Murringen and was on the point of leaving. All of us piled on his jeep and headed for the town. I expected to be killed at any moment of the ride, for the road was under almost constant enemy artillery fire; clusters of shells exploded intermittently on all sides of our creeping vehicle. By God's grace we made it to Murringen unscathed, though the vehicle itself was hit by shell fragments in many places.

An hour later I again sought out Captain Brown. His muddy, bloody, and exhausted troops were digging their foxholes to form a dishearteningly thin defensive line along the military crest of a gentle slope that lay in front of the town. He and I walked the line together in the darkness; we agreed that the situation seemed hopeless; a determined enemy assault would destroy us in no time. But we were mentally prepared to fight to the end.

Around midnight, before the enemy reached Murringen, we were ordered to withdraw to the town of Elsenborn, a distance of some twelve miles. At the twin towns of Krinkelt-Rocherath, which lay between us and Elsenborn, we were informed that enemy tanks had blocked our route, and our regimental commander ordered us to abandon it and move cross-country to our destination. We plodded through deep snow throughout the remainder of the night and reached Elsenborn at midday of the 18th.

The following afternoon we moved into position on a commanding

ridge about a mile east of town. Our first night on the Elsenborn Ridge
was unforgettable. The whistle and crash of bursting shells, ours and
the enemy's, were incessant; the landscape in all directions was aglow
with the fires of burning towns and villages. We worked desperately
throughout the night for we knew the foe would soon be upon us with
renewed fury. We dug foxholes and gun emplacements in the snow and
frozen earth, distributed ammunition and field rations, strung barbed
wire and laid machine guns to crossfire in front of our position, installed
field telephones to the various unit command posts, plotted target areas
for the artillery and mortars, and prepared a medical aid station to receive a fresh harvest of casualties. We were aware that no further withdrawal would be ordered, whatever the circumstances, and I could sense
in the demeanor of the troops at all ranks that this resolution was written in their hearts.

We felt demoralized, disgraced over having been driven from our
original position. Only later did we learn the full significance of our battle at Losheimergraben and other key points along the original line.
The German plan had called for a complete penetration at Losheimergraben the morning of December 16. It took them almost thirty-six
hours to drive us from this position; the delay was fatal to their plans.
Our two days of bitter travail had stalled Hitler's great counteroffensive beyond recovery.

Two of our division's battalions (the 1st Battalion of my regiment
plus two platoons of Capt. Wesley J. Simmons's Company K and Lt.
Lyle Bouck's Intelligence and Reconnaissance Platoon) were awarded
presidential citations for their roles in this resistance. One battalion of
another of the division's regiments received the honor. Doubtless many
other units of the division also deserved it; in my judgment Captain
Brown and his Company L deserved it for their role in stopping the
enemy thrust at the Losheimergraben railway station and guarding the
vulnerable right flank of the regiment and division throughout the day
of the 16th and until ordered to withdraw the following day.

The entire division was decorated by the Belgian government with an
accompanying citation that read "for extraordinary heroism in combat." Hugh Cole lists the stubborn defense of the Losheim Gap by the
99th and 2nd Infantry Divisions as one of the significant reasons for the

failure of the German offensive. John Eisenhower, in his insightful book *The Bitter Woods,* says the occupation and defense of the Elsenborn Ridge by these two divisions may have been the most decisive action of the entire campaign. In an allusion to the battle of Gettysburg, Stephen Ambrose referred to the Elsenborn Ridge as the Little Round Top of the Ardennes campaign.

Perhaps the most meaningful accolade received by my regiment was not at all intended as an accolade. It came from the enemy, from the man considered by Hitler to be the toughest, most resourceful soldier in the Wehrmacht, Col. Otto Skorzeny. His exploits were legendary; he had led the commando raid that rescued Mussolini from the Italian partisans, and the raid that abducted the Hungarian regent, Admiral Miklós Horthy, out of his country. Hitler had personally selected Skorzeny to lead a contingent of commandos in the Ardennes campaign; he and his troops, mounted on vehicles, were to follow the advancing wave of the German attack on Losheimergraben and sweep through the anticipated quick breach in our line. Their primary mission was to seize the bridges on the Meuse River; they were also to sow confusion among us by scattering Germans in American uniforms at key points behind the line.

Skorzeny's memoir reflects his disappointment over the German failure to achieve an immediate breakthrough at Losheimergraben the morning of December 16. He wrote that at noon the "Americans were defending themselves particularly stoutly; the only news was of violent fighting, with no considerable gain [by German troops]."

We remained in position on the Elsenborn Ridge for about six weeks. Enemy mortar and artillery fire came down on us continuously. It became impossible to take a step in the snow without touching one of the ugly, fan-shaped smudges left by the bursting shells. Our own artillery also fired without respite, crippling the enemy and sparing us infantrymen countless casualties. Capt. Henry Reath, our battalion artillery liaison officer, was instrumental in planning a great "time-on-target" bombardment that was credited with breaking up one of the most threatening German attacks before it could be launched.

Our position on the ridge became the hinge of the northern shoulder of the deep bulge in the line that caused the entire battle to be named popularly the "Battle of the Bulge." Eventually it drew scores of American divisions into it and became the greatest, bloodiest battle fought by the American army in World War II.

The weather now became almost as formidable as the Germans. Night after night the thermometer fell below zero Fahrenheit, one night to minus seventeen degrees; it hovered around ten or fifteen degrees above zero in the middle of the day. The wind blew with gale force, driving pellets of snow almost like shot into our faces. Providing hot food on the front line became impossible, and we were obliged to resort to canned emergency rations exclusively. Remaining stationary in the cold, damp foxholes, with physical exercise sharply limited, we began to suffer casualties from trenchfoot, an affliction brought on by inadequate circulation of blood in the extremities.

Trenchfoot in an advanced stage becomes gangrenous. Amputation is then the only remedy. At one point we were losing more men from trenchfoot than from enemy fire. The high command responded with drastic measures. At night, groups of men were to be taken by turns out of the foxholes and made to perform calisthenics. All troops were to change socks and massage and exercise their feet daily for a period of at least thirty minutes. We got clean socks by exchanging the used ones for fresh ones. The used socks were taken back to the kitchen facilities miles behind the lines to be washed and dried and returned to us. This unglamorous but vital laundry and logistical operation went on daily throughout our time on the Elsenborn Ridge.

Lieutenant platoon leaders and platoon sergeants were to visit every foxhole regularly to see that these preventive measures were carried out. Officers were subject to court-martial if an excessive number of trenchfoot cases showed up in their units within a week.

In time the combination of extreme cold, fatigue, hazard, and boredom became maddening. A few men broke under the stress, wetting themselves repeatedly, weeping, vomiting, or showing other alarming physical symptoms. Only with a raging fever was a soldier deemed sick enough for temporary relief from front-line duty. Otherwise, the cure-all APC tablets had to suffice.

Men began to wound themselves one way or another in order to get away from the front. Sometimes this was intentional; sometimes it was caused by a gross negligence that grew out of the prevailing fear, exhaustion, and misery. The most horrendous story I heard about a self-inflicted wound was that of a soldier said to have shattered a hand and arm by lying down next to a large tree, reaching around its trunk, and exploding a grenade in his hand. Soldiers who committed self-inflicted wounds were also subject to court-martial.

At Elsenborn we received replacements for the many losses we had incurred. The procedure for doing this was bizarre. By army policy all units were kept constantly at full roster, or as nearly so as possible. This was done through a complex replacement system, except that the new-comers were not called "replacements." Instead, in a futile effort to avoid further demoralizing them by reminding them that they were taking the places of men who had been killed, wounded, or captured, they were designated by the euphemism "reinforcements."

Only a Kafka could truly describe the depersonalizing effects of the arrangement. Upon arriving in Europe from the basic training centers, the new men were sent, not to "Reinforcement Depots," but to "Re-placement Depots," or "Repple-Depples" as they were promptly dubbed by the soldiers. From here they were sent forward to the divisions on the line. To this point they had no unit assignment, no way of developing either personal friendship or organizational confidence and pride. They were interchangeable parts in the giant machine. Quite possibly some of them died before they had time to learn the names of the men in the foxholes with them. Eventually, we set up a brief behind-the-line orientation program in an effort to solve this problem. Its success was questionable.

The marvel is that the draftee divisions were able to generate and maintain any esprit de corps at all. Formed originally by mixing men indiscriminately from throughout the nation, thus severing all personal, social, community, and regional bonds, identified by anonymous num-bers (394th Infantry Regiment, 99th Infantry Division), and replen-ished through the notorious Repple-Depples, their only source of morale, other than the shared hazard and hardship, was the character and patriotism of the soldiers, rank and file. Fortunately, that proved to be sufficient.

One of my more memorable, if trivial, experiences occurred in mid-January when I received a twenty-four-hour pass to go back to an army rest center in the city of Vervier, Belgium, about twenty-five miles behind the front. The army had taken over a hotel for its purposes. My first act in the town was to visit the commissary and pick up a complete change of clothing; then, because it was near closing time for the mess hall, I hurried there to eat supper.

But what I most eagerly anticipated was the luxury of a slow, voluptuous hot bath. I had not bathed or had my clothing off my body since leaving England well over two months earlier. My garments seemed plastered to my skin. Returning to my room from the mess hall, I prepared for the bath by stripping. Then I turned the faucet to run the water hot in the tub. Vain hope! Others had beaten me to the hot water. To get a bath I would be obliged to take it in unheated water.

I hesitated in a mood of anger and frustration. Because of the scarcity of fuel, the temperature in the hotel was kept just high enough to prevent the plumbing from freezing, barely. In a moment of desperate resolve I took a heavy swig of Scotch whiskey, soaped myself frantically, sucked in a deep breath, and committed myself to the icy water. The shock was indescribable. I couldn't breathe. I wasn't sure I would survive the ordeal. I splashed about frenetically for a few seconds before leaping out onto the floor and drying myself furiously. Then, to my delight, I began to feel as if thousands of tiny electrical charges were shooting through me, warming me to an incandescent glow. I slipped into my fresh, heavy GI long underwear, crawled into bed, and slept like a log for eighteen hours.

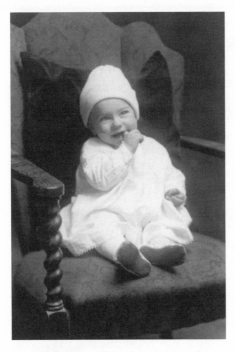

Charles Pierce Roland at nine months

The author as a high school
student

Lieutenant Roland in Natchez

Captain Roland in Gay Paree

In Ochsenfurt, Germany, after
the war in Europe ended

Allie Lee Aycock as a Veterans Administration dietitian in Pineville, Louisiana

Allie Lee and Charles dining at the Peabody Hotel
in Memphis just before their marriage

Wedding announcement in the snow: "Jan. 23 Allie & Chick"

Allie Lee and Charles Roland as newlyweds

Charles, Allie Lee, and son Clifford in the mountains of Virginia

Professor Bell I. Wiley flanked by Otis Singletary (left) and the author

Author and wife at Hitler's great stadium for Nazi rallies in Nuremberg

The author (standing, left) with his parents, Grace and Clifford, and siblings (left to right) Paul, Josephine, Isaac, and Hall C. "Mack"

The Roland children, (left to right) Karen, Charles, and Clifford

The author as president of the Kentucky Civil War Round Table
and Emeritus Alumni Professor at the University of Kentucky

With Gloria and Otis Singletary

With war comrade Samuel Lombardo at a 99th Infantry Division reunion

With Genevieve and Kent Masterson Brown ashore
at Oak Alley Plantation, Louisiana, from the
Mississippi River steamboat *American Queen*

With war comrade Neil Brown at the grave of Lt. Robert Fick
in the Henri Chapelle cemetery in Belgium

Victory in Europe

In combat the battalion S-3 becomes the operations officer. His duties, as described in the field manual, include keeping a situation map showing the disposition of all battalion units and everything that is known of the enemy positions and weapons. He is supposed to have this information at his fingertips at all times in order to be able to advise the battalion commander on tactical matters. In other words, he plays the role of tactical alter ego to the commander. Anytime the battalion makes a move not in actual contact with the enemy, the S-3 carries out a reconnaissance of the routes and the selection of an assembly area, then guides the battalion there. The S-3 is, of course, subject to perform any special missions ordered by the commander.

My battalion commander frequently employed me to bear instructions to the company commanders during combat operations and to observe and report on the situations at the company fronts. Ordinarily the regimental commander sent orders and instructions to the battalion commander by a liaison officer (a lieutenant). But when the regimental commander wished to issue particularly important or complicated instructions and give an opportunity for questions and answers, he called the battalion S-3's back and sent the instructions through them. These occasions were usually taxing experiences for me as I made my way laboriously along roads erupting intermittently with enemy shellfire, through the shattered and deserted villages or the dark and menacing woods at two o'clock in the morning in a blacked-out jeep, accompanied by a couple of sleepy riflemen riding shotgun in the vehicle.

The most important routine extra duty assigned me was that of preparing the heavy-weapons fire plan to support each battalion operation. This involved selecting targets in advance for the artillery and the battalion's heavy machine guns and mortars. In formulating the plans I would consult with Captain Reath, the battalion artillery liaison officer, and Captain Shank of the battalion's heavy-weapons company, Company M. Thus the plans submitted to the battalion commander represented collaborative efforts, and he seldom changed them.

Perhaps the most traumatic episode involving my duties as the battalion operations officer occurred near the end of the Ardennes campaign. The German salient had been almost eliminated, and the divisions on our right were attacking to straighten the line. One night the battalion operations officers of my regiment were summoned back to regimental headquarters for special orders and instructions. Higher authorities had ordered that each of our battalions on the line send out a combat patrol in daylight to give the appearance that our division also was participating in the general American attack. The purpose of this action: to fix in position the enemy in our immediate front and prevent them from shifting troops to meet the attack of our other divisions.

When I conveyed this order to my battalion commander, he decided that the platoon to make the demonstration would come from Company L. Captain Brown was to select the specific platoon. He chose his support platoon, Lt. John Comfort's, and sent him to the battalion command post for instructions. The battalion commander gave him the order, and I gave him the instructions I had received from the regimental commander and told him I would accompany him in a reconnaissance of the terrain.

Accordingly, he and I traversed the entire battalion front under sporadic mortar and machine-gun fire, seeking the most feasible route for his approach. We selected a shallow draw leading down to the woods where the enemy line was located. This route seemed likeliest to shield him and his men from the heaviest volume of enemy fire. When we had finished, I asked, "Do you have any questions?" He replied, "No questions, sir." We gazed momentarily into each other's eyes, both of us fully aware of the suicidal nature of the operation.

It occurred the next morning under murderous enemy fire. Lieutenant Comfort and an inordinate number of the members of his platoon were killed. I earnestly hope they accomplished their mission, that their sacrifice was not in vain. After the passage of more than half a century I can still see the look in his eyes that day when we parted.

The last day of January 1945, still in the dead of winter, we left our maze of dugouts, foxholes, and crawl trenches on the Elsenborn Ridge to take part in the great Allied advance to iron out what remained of the bulge in the line. In this action our troops sustained many casualties from antipersonnel mines as well as from bullets and shells. The mines had been planted under the snow by the Germans as they withdrew and were invisible to our soldiers. They were devilish contrivances that shattered the foot or leg of anyone unlucky enough to step on one of them.

Another remarkably cool and brave act by one of our junior officers occurred in connection with the mines. Here and there, as the troops advanced, a soldier exploded one of them and lay groaning in agony. Lt. Samuel Lombardo's platoon of Company I, 394th Infantry, halted. He was unable to get them moving again when he ordered them forward. Facing his "moment of truth" as an officer, he made his decision. He backed his platoon out and instructed the soldiers to move through the minefield in single file, each man stepping carefully in the footprints of the man in front of him. Lombardo went first. Providentially, he led them through the treacherous area without another casualty. Afterward, his troops would have marched upon his order into the gates of hell, and sometimes did.

After a brief return to our former position on the Elsenborn Ridge, we were sent back into corps reserve for a few days of rest and rehabilitation. We bathed and relaxed. The Red Cross coffee-and-doughnut trucks appeared with pretty girls in charge. How we did enjoy both the refreshments and the company of the girls!

When the break ended we were moved back into the line at Losheimergraben amid the grim mementos of our previous fight there. One of my most nerve-wracking experiences occurred in the occupation of this position. We moved into it at night, replacing a unit from another division. Shortly we received orders that we were to attack at 0600 the following morning; our advance would be preceded by a brief but intense bombardment of the enemy line by our artillery.

There appeared to be a serious problem. When I placed on the battalion situation map the transparent position sketch sent me by the commander of Company I, it indicated that one of his platoons was in the projected artillery impact zone. Lieutenant Colonel Moore (recently promoted to this rank) instructed me to communicate this information to the commander of Company I and have him investigate the situation and take whatever corrective action was needed. The battalion commander then left the command post to visit the other companies as they moved into the line.

Our field telephone line was not yet installed to Company I, and I attempted to get in touch with the company commander by radio, but without success. I then sent a messenger to deliver the information and report back to me. After a considerable lapse of time without any response, I sent a second messenger; again, no response, and no sign of either messenger.

At about midnight Colonel Moore came into the command post. The first thing he said was, "Has the situation of Company I been straightened out?" I told him how it stood. He then looked me searchingly in the face and said, "This must be taken care of. What do you suggest?" I knew what he meant, and replied, "Sir, I will attempt personally to get this information to Company I."

Moore and I were close friends; he had been largely responsible for my promotion to the rank of captain. He was aware that in this undertaking I would be wandering around in the woods in pitch darkness trying to find the lost unit. He said quietly, "You may have any escort you wish for this job. Take an entire platoon from the reserve company if you feel you will need it." I thought the matter over quickly and replied that I would prefer a single soldier to accompany me, and I identified a sergeant from the reserve company as the one I wanted. He had a reputation for fortitude and resourcefulness. He was promptly brought to the command post and briefed on the mission. His reply was as characteristic as it was laconic: "I understand, sir."

We prepared for the mission by blacking our faces and discarding such equipment as packs and canteens that might make noise by catching or striking branches. Then we set out to find the lost company. I'm not ashamed to admit I was frightened: the front line was unstable and porous; we had every reason to believe that we could run afoul of an enemy patrol; or stray into the enemy position; or be mistaken for the enemy by our own troops; or, perhaps most upsetting of all, step on an antipersonnel mine set by the enemy as they withdrew.

The entire affair ended happily. None of the fearsome possibilities occurred; we found Company I after a roam through the woods, in the course of which we encountered Lieutenant Zuber and a telephone wire crew also looking for the lost company. As it turned out, no troops were in the proposed artillery impact zone; the company commander's location sketch, done hastily in the dark, showed the one platoon to be farther forward than it actually was. The sergeant and I returned to the command post at about 0300 hours and conveyed the good news to the battalion commander. Then we sat down to decompress while we sipped hot cocoa from our canteen cups. The artillery opened fire shortly before 0600 and lifted it a few minutes later; the infantry moved forward according to plan; everything was back to normal.

The division now joined the general Allied advance through the Rhineland. At this point I got a lucky break of incredible proportions. It happened this way: I, along with the battalion commander and executive officer, was eating a supper of the usual C-rations in the cellar of a shelled-out house when I was called to the field telephone. The regimental adjutant was on the other end of the line. He informed me that I had received orders to attend a school for regimental education officers and instructed me to report to regimental headquarters at 0600 the next morning with a jeep and driver and all my gear.

I was flabbergasted. I vaguely recalled having been designated the regimental education officer back at Camp Maxey, Texas, an appointment not particularly intended as an honor. Every regiment had been ordered to make such an appointment; I was selected because my records revealed that I had once been a schoolteacher. My duties in garrison were in addition to those as the battalion S-3. They included distributing literature sent down from higher headquarters which was designed to inform the troops on the issues that had brought us into the war and to enhance their morale. I also made brief talks along these lines to assemblies of soldiers. So much had occurred since leaving the United States that I had virtually forgotten the assignment, and I assumed it had ended with our movement overseas and entry into combat.

The adjutant's message did not thrill me. "Where is this to take place?" I inquired grumpily, believing it would occur in some wrecked, unheated building a few miles behind the line. I felt free to reveal my sour mood to the adjutant because we had gone through OCS together and were personal friends. He replied, "Paris, France, you bastard. Do you want to go?" Did I want to go! Does a bear want honey, or a bee want nectar! Tennessee Charlie was on his way to Gay Paree!

We drove all of one day to reach the fabled city. My driver was a handsome, bright young soldier from Ohio. His name was Allen Poese. He was as excited as I was over our mission. Our route took us through many historic sites. As we approached the city of Rheims, its great cathedral, standing on the highest point of land and towering far above its surroundings, became visible from miles away. It seemed to float in the sky like El Greco's painting of Toledo. After we entered the city we sought out the cathedral, drove up to the very door, and went in. We found ourselves in semidarkness and tomblike silence. The massive columns supporting the towering ceiling stood out like redwood trunks of alabaster. Candles burned in the alcoves; the smell of incense hung in the still air. A feeling of mystery and awe came over us, and we returned to our jeep without speaking.

We had another emotional experience on the way to Paris. Coming upon a marker indicating a side road to an American cemetery, we turned off the main highway, drove perhaps a mile, and found ourselves at a cemetery and chapel for American doughboys who fell in World War I. We stood in respectful silence and surveyed the neat grounds and white crosses arranged like troops in a review formation. As we drove on toward our destination we discussed the fates that had brought both those soldiers and us to this hallowed spot so far from home. Unspoken, but present, was the keen awareness that one or both of us might end up in just such a place.

We reached Paris at dusk. The streets were lit and teeming with people. We marveled at the graceful architecture and statuary that stood on every side. We marveled even more at the throngs of pretty women who appeared to us to be dressed in high fashion. The contrast between these scenes and those of death and destruction on the front was almost unbearable; it gave an impression of passing from hell to heaven in an instant. In a mood of almost tantric delight we sought out our assigned quarters and settled in for a week of adventure.

I learned that the army was planning to create a school in each regiment when the war was over. The regimental education officer would organize and run the school. The purpose of our being in Paris was to receive instructions on how to go about doing this. We were in class each day until noon. The rest of the twenty-four hours belonged to us. We made the most of it.

During the afternoons I rode the subway to all of the historic places in Paris that I knew about, including the Louvre, the cathedral of Notre Dame, and Napoleon's tomb. I went by trolley to the historic and spectacular site Versailles. At night I visited the less-historic but no-less-famous spots: the Lido, Moulin Rouge, Bal Tabourin, and the Folies Bergères. I found the music and dancing electrifying and the dancers' costumes (or virtual lack thereof) both shocking and intriguing. The citizens were wonderfully hospitable to their American liberators, particularly to those with a generous supply of cigarettes. I came to understand fully the sentiments of the popular World War I song that said, "How ya gonna keep 'em down on the farm after they've seen Paree?"

A day or two before the end of my Paris excursion, I carried out a mission my mother had been urging for some time: I had my picture taken. She wanted a photograph of me made in Europe, one similar to the likeness of my uncle Lee Jackson Roland that had been made there during World War I. Walking down a Paris street one day and sighting a sign that read "Photographie," I entered the establishment under it and found myself in an extremely narrow, dingy, cluttered shop. From somewhere in the back of it emerged a wizened, tubercular-looking, unkempt little Frenchman of perhaps sixty years of age. He wore a shapeless, grimy beret set at an angle on his head and dangled an incredibly evil-smelling cigarette from his lips.

I was able to convey my wishes in halting French. He mumbled a reply and motioned for me to be seated on a high stool. He disappeared for a moment under the cowl of an immense box-shaped camera that looked as if it were a relic of the Franco-Prussian War of 1870–1871, pointed to an upper corner of the ceiling, said "Regardez," then set off a powder flash that filled the room with smoke. I paid him with cigarettes—the most prized currency owned by American soldiers in Europe—and gave him my army mailing address. I seriously doubted that I would ever see the finished product. This did him an injustice; the pictures arrived several weeks later, after the war in Europe had ended. He turned out to be a master photographer; they were the best pictures of me ever taken.

At the end of the school we returned to our unit. This was not easy, for we were obliged to track it down through the ruined cities and towns of the Rhineland. We caught up with it the day it reached the city of Dormagen near the Rhine and thirty or forty miles north of Cologne.

Here I witnessed what was to me perhaps the most unsettling sight of the war: death at random among the civilian population. Though Dormagen had not been bombed from the air and was relatively un-damaged by the war, the day we entered the town it was shelled by the artillery of both sides as the Germans withdrew across the Rhine. The bombardments apparently caught the inhabitants by surprise as they went about their daily affairs, outside of the stonewalled cellars in which they customarily took refuge. They suffered many casualties.

In passing through the town I came upon a small hospital or clinic that was overwhelmed with the wounded. The surrounding grounds were covered with dozens, possibly scores, of dead bodies. Among them were men in business suits, women in street attire, and children in their school clothes. They showed every imaginable kind of wound; some of them lay with brains or intestines spilling out on the neatly mown grass. My eyes fell upon a golden-haired little girl who bore a shocking re-semblance to the one I had kissed while in the first grade. I was by now accustomed to death in uniform, and steeled to it, but I turned away from this surreal and ghastly tableau with a feeling of revulsion, horror, and remorse.

But battle-conditioned soldiers do not dwell at length on death in any guise. We quickly went about establishing quarters for the night. Spring was in the air; a great river lay between us and the remnants of the German army; the war seemed to be winding down. We heard that somewhere south of us one of our armored divisions had captured an in-tact bridge across the Rhine. A holiday mood began to spread among all ranks. A few soldiers carried out an old promise by walking down to the bank of the river and making a direct, personal contribution to its volume and ammonia content.

The holiday mood halted abruptly when fresh orders arrived from corps headquarters, and an hour or two later we were on trucks, riding through the night, destination unknown. At some time well after midnight we stopped and established a bivouac in an open field. I was awakened at dawn with orders to report to division headquarters to join another advance party. We rode in jeeps for five or six miles, then walked for a few hundred yards and stopped at the top of a bluff. Below us lay the Rhine. Spanning its broad current was a bridge with a cantilevered superstructure. Our maps told us that the town at the near end of the bridge was Remagen. We were looking at the captured Ludendorff railroad bridge.

Later that day I had an opportunity to get a close-up view of the bridge. Posted on the superstructure at the near end was an indifferently lettered sign that read boastfully but fittingly, "Cross the Rhine with dry feet, compliments of the 9th Armored Division." That night, beginning at midnight, we crossed the historic river with dry feet.

As we stepped onto the bridge, I recalled with something like awe that, two thousand years earlier, Caesar crossed the same stream at almost the same spot to fight the same enemy. The whistle and crash of hostile artillery shells brought my reverie to a quick end. Walking forward suddenly became difficult; each shell seemed aimed directly at my chest. Fortunately the bridge was not hit, but the shells inflicted many casualties on our troops as they approached it. All had been quiet until the head of the column reached the bridge; then the German bombardment began. We were convinced that someone in the town was somehow signaling the enemy gunners.

We entered the line a short distance south of the bridge. I am informed that ours was the first complete Allied infantry division across the river, though parts of some other divisions were already fighting in the bridgehead. The mission of the force was to enlarge the bridgehead so that our armor could break out of it. My battalion was attacking south (upstream), with our right flank on the river.

The first day of this fighting was in certain ways the most eventful day of the war for me personally, the day on which I believe I made my most important contributions to the efficiency of the battalion. The first of the episodes which made the day unusual for me was that of being subjected to a heavy bombardment by our own artillery. Our battalion advance had moved through the village of Ariendorf, and our artillery liaison officer, Captain Reath, and I had just entered the village when the rounds began to fall on it. Reath, standing at his jeep with admirable courage and presence of mind as the shells burst around him, radioed furiously to have the firing halted. After perhaps thirty seconds, which seemed like an eternity, he was successful. An awful lot of shells can fall in that amount of time, particularly if the observer is the recipient of them.

The other personal events occurred either directly or indirectly because of an unusual situation that developed in the battalion command.

Customarily, if the battalion commander was absent from the command post, the battalion executive officer would be there to make the decisions. But the primary routine responsibility of the executive officer was running the battalion's administrative affairs: supply, medical treatment, evacuation, and communications. On this occasion, the administrative affairs were extraordinarily difficult because of the great volume of traffic pouring across the bridge and becoming jammed into a limited space on the east bank with inadequate roads leading to the front line. The scene was one of bedlam, with enemy shells and bombs exploding all over, and our own antiaircraft guns filling the sky with their furious bursts. For several hours this day the executive officer was away from the command post working hard to unsnarl the traffic, keep our supplies flowing, and see to the evacuation of the wounded.

Meanwhile, the battalion commander was trailing one of the rifle companies in the advance. He ordinarily stayed in touch with the command post by radio or field telephone, which was kept operative by reeling out the wire as he and his party moved forward. But this day he was completely out of touch with the command post for several hours because he and his party were pinned down in a ditch by enemy fire, which killed the two officers who were with him, Lt. Robert Fick and Lt. Samuel Graf. Both were friends of mine, Fick an especially close friend; he was the battalion intelligence officer at the time of his death, and he had been a platoon leader in Company I when I was the commander of it.

An exceptionally stressful event for me developed that morning in the absence of both the battalion commander and the executive officer. Captain Brown got me on the phone or radio with an urgent request for heavy mortar fire on an enemy machine gun that was inflicting casualties on one of his platoons. He had already called directly to the batteries for both artillery fire and heavy mortar fire, but both had been denied because our information in the command post said that another of our companies, K, had already occupied the position; fire on it would fall on our own troops. Brown insisted indignantly that he was correct in his location of the German gun and that my information from Company K was wrong.

The battalion commander or executive officer, or I as the commander's deputy, could approve Brown's request. I had to make a decision, and I was in a terrible quandary. But I trusted Brown's judgment, and Company K was operating under a temporary commander, a first lieutenant, because the regular commander was absent on another assignment. Maybe the acting company commander had misread his location on the map. With a lump the size of a grapefruit in my belly, I ordered our 81-mm mortars to deliver the fire as Brown requested. They did so and silenced the enemy weapon. Brown had been right; his troops, and my "bacon," were saved.

Another unusual happening occurred that day: we received a platoon of African American troops. In the army's frantic search for riflemen to replace the losses of the Ardennes battle, General Eisenhower had authorized the formation of platoons of African American volunteers from the noncombat branches. They were to be commanded by white lieutenants. Each front-line infantry regiment was to get one of these platoons; ours had been assigned to Company K. It arrived at a timely moment; a gap had developed in our line between Companies L and K. I personally placed the platoon so as to cover the gap.

There was widespread doubt that these troops would fight effectively. An African American division in Italy, the 92nd Infantry, had performed poorly. I shared the doubts about the capabilities of these soldiers. I am pleased to report that the new platoon served out the remainder of the European war with our battalion and that they fought well.

Throughout much of the day, Captain Brown had repeatedly complained that the right flank of his company was dangerously exposed. "Where the hell is Company K?" he kept asking me. Something obviously was wrong with that unit. As soon as the executive officer came into the battalion command post, I reported the situation. He ordered me to go to Company K, identify the problem, and do what I judged appropriate to correct it. When I informed Brown what I was about to do, his reply was, "That's the best goddamned news I've heard all day."

The moment I arrived at the Company K command post I saw what was wrong. The lieutenant who was serving as the temporary commander had been hit by an enemy bullet that penetrated his helmet, front and rear, and grazed the side of his head, leaving a long bloody streak in its track. His "bell" had been thoroughly rung and clearly was still ringing; he was in a stupor, his eyes glazed, his mouth sagging open. I ordered him back to the battalion aid station with a rifleman to escort him. I remained with Company K long enough to talk the situation over with the company first sergeant, who appeared to possess a cool head and a strong presence of mind. I then appointed the platoon leader recommended by him to take charge as the temporary company commander. After discussing the situation carefully with the lieutenant, I returned to the battalion command post. Afterward the company seemed to operate effectively.

Late that same day I experienced what I believe were my closest brushes with death in the war. They occurred in the following way. For some reason our battalion antitank platoon had fallen behind the battalion advance. The executive officer sent me back to find it and bring it up. Just after my jeep cleared the village of Ariendorf and turned into the highway toward our rear, I observed the members of the antitank platoon lying prone in a ditch that ran beside the road. Ordering my driver to halt, I was about to address the platoon sergeant when he shouted, "Captain, this road is under fire." At that moment I became aware of staccato popping sounds, of bullets ricocheting past me from behind, and of tracers striking the pavement in front. One bullet from behind passed between the driver and me and struck the dashboard in front of our faces. A plume of smoke shot up from beneath the jeep's hood; the engine died instantly.

I piled out of my side of the vehicle, the driver out of his. We wriggled frantically into the ditch with the other soldiers. After being there a few moments, I said to the sergeant, "We've got to knock out that enemy gun." He replied that he was attempting to do so, that he had a 60-mm mortar set to fire but had been unable to locate the offending weapon. I could see the mortar in the ditch about 100 feet behind us.

After a pause, I committed a foolish act that almost did me in for the second time. I clambered up to the floodwall that ran parallel to the ditch, placed my hands on top of the wall, pulled myself up, and gingerly poked my head above it to try to locate the gun. I hoped the twigs and leaves I was wearing on my helmet for camouflage would deceive the enemy. They didn't. Explosions from their rapid-fire 20-mm antiaircraft shells suddenly burst all around me. One of the shells hit the top of the wall near my head; I momentarily blacked out and fell back into the ditch. The next thing I knew clearly, the sergeant was pressing me back with both his hands on my chest and saying, "Stay down, Captain, you've been hit."

At that moment a series of four or five terrific explosions occurred just on the other side of the floodwall. At first I believed they came from enemy artillery fire and feared that the next salvo would land among us in the ditch. I was quickly relieved by hearing excited and joyous shouts in English that arose from beyond the wall; the explosions were from the 90-mm cannon of one of our tank destroyers, which had sighted the enemy gun and blasted it into Kingdom Come. I sent up a quick prayer of thanksgiving.

As it turned out, I was not badly hurt: nothing more than some lacerations from shell fragments on the fingers of my left hand. The sergeant bandaged my hand, and I went about my business, though for a few days my fingers were badly swollen and stiff, and both the battalion surgeon and I suspected they might be broken. They were not. But it was an exceedingly close call for me; if I had been a fraction of a second later in ducking my head below the top of the wall, the shell fragments probably would have gone into my brain.

That night I reported to the battalion aid station, where an aid man cleaned and dressed my hand and administered the required tetanus booster shot. My memory of the place is inerasable. Located in a deep cellar, it was lit by gasoline lanterns suspended from hooks screwed into the overhead beams. Lining the floor on litters with narrow aisles between were a score or more of wounded soldiers. They lay quiet, their pain eased by morphine or shock, or both. All were heavily bandaged, a face, a head, a limb, a torso. Plastic tubes extended to many of them from bottles of blood plasma that hung from the hilts of bayonets which had been thrust point-down between the cobblestones of the floor. The surgeon and his assistants worked ceaselessly among them.

They were out of the fray. One of them pointed to a taped leg and said, "Look, Captain, a million-dollar wound," which, either in sport or in earnest, we called a wound that was serious enough to remove one from combat but not serious enough to be fatal or permanently disabling. In one corner lay a group of soldiers whose faces were covered with blankets. They had given, in Abraham Lincoln's exalted words, the "last full measure of devotion."

The most memorable nonbattle episode of the Remagen operation involved Lombardo's platoon flag. He was an Italian immigrant who had arrived in the United States as a boy of nine, and he felt a burning sense of American patriotism. Earlier he had requested an American flag to be displayed by his platoon and had been told that none was available. He decided to make one. Beginning with a commandeered white sheet, he and his platoon rounded up red and blue cloth and thread, located scissors and a sewing machine, cut out the stars and stripes, and made a United States flag. One side only was finished when we reached the Rhine, but it was probably the first American or Allied national emblem to be flown east of that river in World War II. The other side of the flag was finished later. Lombardo's platoon flag is now in the possession of the Infantry School museum at Fort Benning, Georgia.

After the breakout from the Remagen bridgehead, the 99th Division was picked up on trucks, hauled some sixty miles northeast in Germany, and placed in line on the back side of the Ruhr Pocket, in which an entire enemy army of more than 300,000 troops was trapped. After fighting for about two weeks, we participated in taking the surrender of that army, the greatest bag of prisoners ever taken in one action by an American force. After many weeks of mortal struggle with the Germans, during which time we actually caught only fleeting glimpses of them, the sight of such a multitude directly in front of our eyes was startling.

As we entered one of the towns that we captured in that operation, I got a call from Captain Brown, who rather breathlessly said, "Come up here, there is something you would find interesting." I joined him as quickly as possible. What he wanted to show me was a large building filled with young German women in various stages of pregnancy. Communicating with them in German, he had learned that this was a home for selected young women of outstanding Aryan characteristics who had been mated to selected German soldiers of like qualities. In other words, it was an incubator of future Nazis. The inmates, many of them of striking appearance, swarmed about us, preening flirtatiously. An arresting sight!

One of the lighter episodes of my combat experience occurred during the fighting in the Ruhr Pocket. I, along with Reath and Zuber, entered a German house and found a teenage girl standing at the kitchen stove frying potato chips in a large skillet. Suddenly, we heard the whistle of "incoming mail," our name for enemy artillery shells. We threw ourselves down on the kitchen floor to avoid being struck by shell fragments that might fly through the windows. The girl cook disappeared in a flash down the stairs to the cellar where, we later learned, the rest of the family was cowering.

Zuber calmly reached up, grasped the handle of the skillet, took a handful of the fries, and passed them to Reath and me. After a few minutes of quiet the girl reappeared. She indicated no emotion when she saw the empty utensil, but patiently replenished it from a supply in the pantry and began the frying operation again. Hardly was it finished when another salvo of shells came zooming in. Again she disappeared; again we emptied the skillet. I suppose this would have repeated itself all day except we were soon filled up and became tired of the game.

As we departed we handed the frustrated young cook a few American cigarettes. For the first time her stolid expression changed as she broke into a broad, toothy smile; nothing brought greater pleasure than American cigarettes to the addicted and deprived population of Europe. I could readily understand their preference; I never tried one of their ersatz cigarettes, but the smoke from them smelled like dog excrement.

The German civilians in the path of our advance kept themselves as much out of the way as possible. Though their army continued to resist, the civilians did not. They immediately began the practice of hanging white sheets or towels from their windows as tokens of submission. One of these served as the backing for Lombardo's flag. Soon the smaller towns, most of which had not been wrecked by our bombers, began to send out a surrender delegation comprising the bürgermeister (mayor) and a few other selected individuals as we approached. They invariably disavowed the Nazi atrocities and denied any previous knowledge of them.

Two events that I shall never forget occurred during the Ruhr Pocket campaign. One was our receipt of the news of President Franklin D. Roosevelt's death of a paralytic stroke in Warm Springs, Georgia. Americans of a later period have no way of appreciating the impact of this news on the minds and hearts of the wartime generation. He was the leader who had guided the nation through the Great Depression and up to the moment of victory in the war. He had been president since I was a young teenager. I seriously wondered how the nation could go on without him. I suspect most of my fellow soldiers wondered the same thing.

The other event of great import to me personally took place on the anniversary of my birth, April 8. That day my friend Captain Brown was severely wounded by shell fragments that riddled both of his legs. I vividly remember him as he sat on a litter in the battalion command post with his little wool helmet liner cocked at a jaunty angle on his head. He was liberally sedated with morphine and feeling no pain; he sat smoking cigarettes continuously, chatting and laughing with all of us as he waited to be evacuated to the field hospital. He did not say he was the recipient of a "million-dollar" wound, but I suspect he felt that way about it at the moment. I would not see him again for more than forty years. Living in Oregon now, he telephones me every April 8 and we reminisce over our experiences in the war.

Immediately upon the end of hostilities in the Ruhr Pocket, the 99th Division was transferred to the 3rd U.S. Army (the famed General Patton's army) and ordered to join that force deep in Bavaria. We moved by a gigantic truck convoy almost three hundred miles, rolling through the mountains of rubble that had previously been the proud cities of Germany.

An unusual experience awaited me in Bamberg, some forty miles north of Nuremberg. Intrigued by Europe's great medieval cathedrals, I explored all of them I had an opportunity to explore, and I had such an opportunity in Bamberg. When I entered the cathedral there, it was typically dark and silent. Then suddenly it was filled with majestic organ tones from what I guessed was a Bach composition. As I came to the very front of the sanctuary, I was dumbfounded to see at the console, not a German in church attire, but an American soldier in private's uniform. Our army was an amazingly ecumenical organization.

We went into battle formation two or three days' march above the upper Danube River and at the end of April crossed that historic stream on pontoon bridges constructed under fire by the division engineers. We suffered our last serious number of casualties during this operation, most of them from enemy mortar fire. We were keenly disappointed in the appearance of the muddy, smelly river with its shallow banks that gave way to dun pasturelands spreading back as far as the eye could see. It certainly was no "Beautiful Blue Danube" from our vantage point, and the soldiers quickly responded with a crude parody of Johann Strauss Jr.'s waltz tribute to it.

My last combat contribution of any particular significance (or so I perceived it) occurred in the Danube crossing. In order to deceive the enemy as to the location of the crossing, the division made feints at a number of places. The actual crossing was to be led by the regiment downstream from us, to our left. The advance infantry crossing would be made during the night in rubber boats; the engineers would lay a pontoon bridge as soon as a bridgehead had been established on the other side of the stream.

The bridge was to be constructed about a thousand yards down from the village where our battalion command post was located. Our orders were to deliver covering fire for the initial infantry crossing and the building of the bridge. My own orders were, as usual, to prepare a heavy-weapons fire plan to be contained in the order of the battalion commander.

The terrain on the other side of the river was open and clearly visible for a width of several hundred yards, enabling me to make a meticulous visual reconnaissance of the area. My recommended plan assigned artillery and mortar targets to a number of small barns and large haystacks that were capable of concealing enemy weapons. At a distance of about five hundred yards directly across from us stood a small but thick copse of trees which I assigned as the primary target of the tank destroyer that was attached to our battalion. The lieutenant commanding the destroyer marked the spot in the street where he wished it to be positioned, took a compass bearing on the trees, and made a careful estimation of the range to them; but he kept his destroyer hidden behind a house until dark and moved it into position during the night.

Just after dawn the next morning an enemy gun in the copse of trees opened fire on the engineers, who were busy placing their pontoons in the water. The first shell exploded about fifty yards beyond its target. Given three or four seconds in which to adjust range, the gunners would in all probability have hit their mark with the following shots. They never got them off; before they had time to make adjustments our tank destroyer blasted the grove of trees with half a dozen high-explosive rounds. Afterward, the trees stood smoking but silent; the engineers went about their business. I felt quite proud of myself.

We pressed rapidly south after passing the Danube and reached Moosburg on the Isar River the following night. Here an emotional experience awaited us: we liberated an immense prisoner of war camp where many of our former division soldiers captured in the Ardennes were incarcerated. I spent most of the night talking with a young lieutenant who had been a platoon leader in Company I when I was the commander of the unit at Camp Maxey, Texas. He had then been one of the most carefree persons I had ever known: a quintessential playboy. Now he was pensive and somber; I could hardly believe he was the same man. I have been forever thankful for being spared his experience.

We were approaching the Inn River when, on May 7, the war in Europe formally ended. I recall some shouting and firing of weapons into the air to salute the occasion. But there was actually not much display of emotion. The formal cessation of hostilities came as no surprise; the war had been winding down for days with virtually no organized resistance on our front. Besides, we were too weary to kindle much of a celebratory mood. I spent much of the day on my back, prostrated by a severe migraine headache, a malady that had afflicted me from time to time since I was a teenager. It had not attacked me throughout the rigors of military training or the hardships and hazards of combat. Then, in the day of victory and surcease, it returned and laid me low.

After a few days in this position we were again loaded on trucks and hauled back some two hundred miles to an occupation area on the Main River near Würzburg. Our battalion headquarters was located in the town of Ochsenfurt, on the north bank of the river. Here we enjoyed a few months of marvelously relaxed and pleasant living. We were surrounded by an undulating countryside of vineyards and pastures; our occupation duties were more token than real; we spent lots of time playing volleyball and swimming in the Main. From an immense nearby establishment of displaced persons (Poles, Estonians, Latvians, and Lithuanians) we secured servants for our kitchens and quarters; we also secured musicians and dancers for our entertainment.

As the designated regimental education officer, I spent much of my duty time setting up the soldiers' school planned by our authorities and in preparation for which I had been sent to Paris the preceding March. I sent out questionnaires and selected personnel for a faculty; arranged a curriculum of courses and enrolled interested soldiers in them; and sought out school buildings, desks, blackboards, and other educational equipment and supplies. Just as we were ready to begin instruction, the military authorities adopted a policy that completely undercut the entire arrangement; the school never opened.

It never opened because in the early summer 1945 the army in Europe began a comprehensive reorganization and relocation of its troops. It established a classification of soldiers according to time in service, time overseas, receipt of campaign ribbons and Purple Heart medals for wounds, and number of dependents. Each soldier received a certain number of points for each of these. Those soldiers holding above a given number of points were eligible for redeployment to the United States (in other words, they would be sent home); those holding below a given number of points were eligible for redeployment to the Pacific Theater of Operations (to participate in the war against Japan); those holding a number of points between the upper and lower limits were eligible to remain temporarily in the army of occupation. One soldier who initially had a low number of points received news that his wife had delivered triplets, giving him enough points to go home immediately. Deliriously happy, he ran around shouting and waving the telegram in the air. I fell in the classification to remain in the army of occupation.

This general reorganization resulted in the deactivation of the draftee divisions in Europe and the reallocation of their eligible troops into the regular army divisions. In midsummer the 99th Division was deactivated and I was transferred to the 1st Infantry Division along with many of my friends and acquaintances. The 1st Infantry Division had been selected as the security and service force for the Nuremberg trial of the

German war criminals. For about two weeks we were stationed in the city of Ansbach, some forty miles west of Nuremberg.

My most interesting experience while stationed in Ansbach was that of participating in the selection of the Nuremberg buildings where the trials were to occur. For reasons unknown to me I was chosen to be a member of the detail for this mission. We rode in vehicles from Ansbach to Nuremberg. The commanding general of the division rode at the head of the column in his command car with a two-star flag flying at the front. As the lowest-ranking member of the detail, I rode in a jeep at the tail of the column. We had no difficulty in selecting a building because we never disagreed with the general in his judgment. The place selected had been damaged by the fighting, all its windows broken and here and there a gaping shellhole in the walls. After it was suitably patched it served its purpose admirably.

Soon after joining the 1st Division, I got a most lucky break in being chosen to attend a school for several weeks at the University of Dijon in the French city of that name. This came about through an arrangement between the U.S. Army and a number of French universities in which they set up special courses for selected soldiers who were competent in the French language. We received lectures in French on the subjects of French history and culture. Fortunately, the lectures were given deliberately, repetitively, and in quite elementary French.

Of course, the most educational part of the experience was that of living for a period in the French environment. Dijon is famous as a center of the production of mustard; it is also the key city of the department of Burgundy, renowned for the wine that bears its name. Dijon was the historic capital of the medieval duchy of Burgundy, which under the feudal system was a part of France but which for a time was actually stronger than the kingdom of France. In practical terms, this meant the dukes of Burgundy could raise more money and more troops than could the king of France. The haughty dukes lie buried in the crypt of the church of St. Bénigne in Dijon.

Our instructors supplemented their lectures by conducting us on trips to historic sites out of Dijon, including a number of medieval castles and churches. One of the most interesting of these sites was the ancient abbey of Vézelay, where St. Bernard of Clairvaux inspired the king of France to lead a crusade for the freedom of the Holy Land. Another fascinating excursion took us to the celebrated winery of Beaune, where we descended into the immense storage cellar with its maze of seemingly endless corridors stacked high with casks of Burgundy and from which we emerged on the opposite side of the town.

I loved the social atmosphere of Dijon, that of southern France. At night its sidewalk cafés came alive with wine, music, and dancing in the streets. After more than half a century I can still see and hear the little musical band on the balcony and its vocalists rendering their melodious and lighthearted songs. My favorite, which they played and sang over and over, was "Le Petit Vin Blanc." I shall always remember Dijon.

The most momentous event that occurred during my stay in Dijon took place on the other side of the world, but it radically affected my future as well as the world's. This was the explosion of the atomic bombs at Hiroshima and Nagasaki and the immediate Japanese surrender that followed. I was immensely gratified over this turn of affairs; no longer was there the threat that I would be required to fight in the conquest of the Japanese homeland.

When I returned to my assignment with the 1st Infantry Division, its headquarters were in Nuremberg; my office and quarters were in the adjacent city of Furth. My duties were boring beyond description. My official time was spent making surveys of warehouses and other buildings that might be useful to our army and conducting investigations of court-martial charges for such minor violations as reckless driving of vehicles, drunkenness, and disorderly conduct by the troops.

At one point in the late fall I was appointed temporarily to the position of executive officer of my battalion, with my office located in the building next to the one where the war criminals were housed. This gave me an opportunity to get a glimpse of them through a tiny window that was supposed to be blacked out but wasn't. I saw them when they were brought out into the courtyard for physical exercise. The only one I could recognize was Hermann Goering, who appeared to be both arrogant and jovial. Most were later convicted and hanged, but he cheated the noose, allegedly by bribing an American officer to slip him a capsule of poison which he used to commit suicide.

The social life in Nuremberg went a good way toward compensating for the dreariness of my duties. The city buzzed with activity in preparation for the upcoming trial. Large numbers of young women secretaries and administrative assistants arrived from the United States and the other allied countries. My close friend Captain Shank was appointed manager of the refurbished Nuremberg hotel, with its spacious dining room and ballroom and its commodious bar. He found German musicians and performers and staged engaging floor shows two or three times each evening. My relationship with him gave me certain advantages in securing reservations for dinner and dancing at the hotel.

There were other diversions at Nuremberg. We converted the giant stadium where Hitler had held his spectacular Nazi rallies into an American football stadium in which teams from the various occupation army divisions held contests. At a much higher cultural level, our authorities assisted the Germans in cobbling together a symphony orchestra made up of groups of musicians, some from the Berlin symphony, who had been scattered by the war. The orchestra performed in the patched-up Nuremberg opera house, which is where I heard my first live symphony.

An especially thrilling episode was a trip to Berchtesgaden, Hitler's mountain resort, which I made in company with Captain Reath. We stayed in the small but luxurious hotel where the Führer's companions had stayed when they visited him. The hotel had been taken over by our army and was being used as a rest and recreation facility for our troops. We were wined and dined, and entertained by a Bavarian musical band with a company of singers and dancers.

We visited the nearby Königssee, a mountain lake of incomparable beauty, its water so crystalline that individual pebbles were clearly distinguishable at immense depths, and with sheer rock walls rising thousands of feet above the surface, waterfalls cascading down their faces. We also visited Hitler's mountaintop domicile, which had been destroyed by our invading troops, and we collected souvenirs in the form of fragments of stone from its shattered fireplace.

While on the trip to Berchtesgaden, we drove to Salzburg. The most interesting spot we visited in the city was the house where the great composer Mozart had grown up and which now housed a Mozart museum. Especially fascinating was a series of dioramas vividly depicting scenes from his operas.

The presence of the leading figures in the Nuremberg trial added an atmosphere of interest and excitement to the affairs at the hotel. On one occasion I was in a group that listened to Associate Supreme Court

Justice Robert Jackson, the chief American prosecutor in the trial, as he discussed the preparations for it. He, of course, spoke in general terms, not divulging any specific plans, but he made clear that the court would apply established legal procedures. I did not actually witness any of the trial, and I left Nuremberg before it ended.

In early December I received orders returning me to the United States for separation from active military duty. In making the trip from Germany to the port of departure, Marseilles, I had the rare treat of traveling in a "40 and 8," the functional name of the French rail freight cars, each of which would accommodate forty soldiers or eight horses. It contained no seats; the floor was covered with several inches of straw. The weather was cold, and as I recall, the car was heated by a single potbellied stove. We sort of rotated our positions in the car to avoid either stifling or freezing. The trip required three or four days; we ate K-rations—improved field rations that included processed meat, cheese, and a fruit bar—three meals a day. The sanitary facilities consisted of a few communal buckets with an occasional opportunity for emptying them.

The major excitement of the trip occurred when we stopped for about half an hour beside a similar troop train in the railyard of some city. The soldiers on the other train were newcomers from the United States sent as replacements in the army of occupation. An exchange of acid remarks between the two groups would soon have led to a massive brawl if one of the trains had not begun blowing its shrill whistle, signaling it was about to pull out. Fortunately, no blood was shed.

We spent a few days in an immense embarkation-debarkation camp on a high plateau a few miles outside Marseilles, which was visible from the camp. My most unusual experience while there occurred in serving as officer of the guard for one period of twenty-four hours. What made the affair unusual was the presence of several million dollars in currency to be used as the payroll for the troops. The money was contained in boxes that were stacked from floor to ceiling in the guard quarters. I was required to sign for it, though obviously I had no opportunity to count it.

To add zest to the occasion, I was told that Marseilles was the Chicago of France; that the city swarmed with armed gangs, any one of which might attempt a raid on the camp payroll. I relayed this information seriously to the guards before posting them. I slept fitfully in the guard quarters with a loaded carbine and pistol at hand and visited the guard posts frequently throughout the night. Morning came at last with the payroll intact, and I was soon able to turn it over to the succeeding officer of the guard, who appeared to be as nervous as I had been.

A few days later we boarded ship for home. That night as we glided along the smooth surface of the Mediterranean, I lay for hours on a blanket spread on the deck, gazing at the stars which seemed much closer and more luminous than I had ever seen them. I had the feeling that I could almost reach up and touch them.

Countless emotions surged through me as I recalled my tumultuous experiences of the recent past. For a while I lay in somber reflection contemplating a vision of Charlie Allen, Bob Fick, Chaplain Hampton, and other friends reposing among the thousands of graves aligned row on row in the great Henri Chapelle military cemetery that I had learned was located between the Belgian villages of Aubel and Henri Chapelle, the very spot where our regiment had spent the snowy night before moving into the line at Losheimergraben. An image from my early youth floated into my mind, an image of a bronze plaque at the Shiloh battlefield cemetery, and of the haunting words of the verse embossed on its face:

> On fame's eternal camping ground
> Their silent tents are spread
> And glory guards with solemn round
> The bivouac of the dead.

Then the reality of the present moment began to sink in. I was going home! Going home alive and whole! How unimaginably fortunate I had been! An involuntary and unspoken prayer of thanksgiving ascended from me.

The return voyage across the Atlantic was rough, and the ship I was on this time was no *Queen Mary*. My old nemesis, seasickness, revisited me with a vengeance. I fought it off by popping Dramamine pills until I was in a zombielike trance. We landed at Newport News, Virginia, the day before Christmas; I went by troop train to Fort Knox, Kentucky, where I was mustered out of service a few days later.

Civilian Life, Graduate School, and Marriage

My parents were, of course, overjoyed to have me home. At times during the fighting, when the mail from the front was delayed, they had almost given up hope of seeing me alive again. Now I was back, and they could not do enough to please me. My mother prepared enormous meals of my favorite foods and I ate them gluttonously. At midmorning I drank a chocolate malted milk shake at the old-fashioned, marble-topped soda fountain of the City Drug Store; at midafternoon I drank another. In the evenings I was out with boyhood friends drinking beer. At midnight I raided my mother's pantry and refrigerator and washed down half a box of vanilla wafers with a quart of super-rich milk. I loafed blissfully. How heavenly it was to have absolutely nothing to do!

I gained weight at an unbelievable rate. When the war in Europe ended I weighed 150 pounds; after six months at home I weighed 188. Making matters much worse, because of the extreme shortage of civilian clothing I was obliged to wear my uniform; soon the blouse and top of the trousers could not be buttoned. When eventually I received two civilian suits measured and ordered from a Louisville tailor while I was at the Fort Knox separation center, they were so tight on me that I could hardly walk.

Ultimately I began to suspect what I now strongly believe was true: I was in a state of mild depression brought on by my sudden descent from the powerful intoxication of war into the mind-numbing banality and boredom of everyday life in small-town America. I had seen much of the world go up in flames, had participated in the greatest crusade in history, had many times escaped death by a shadow, had been moved by an urgent sense of mission. Suddenly, all this was gone. The only excitement left was to eat, drink, and be merry.

I then learned what many before me have learned: that these activities, however pleasant at first, eventually begin to pall. I needed to get busy somehow. Before leaving Europe I knew that the United States Congress had enacted a measure for providing financial support for veterans to go to school, the so-called GI Bill of Rights. Though I entertained vague intentions of taking advantage of the opportunity, I had made no move to do so. In the fall of 1946 I began to think seriously about entering law school or graduate school, probably at my alma mater, Vanderbilt. But these thoughts came too late for me to enroll for the fall semester.

One day in the midst of this quandary I received a formal notice from my prewar employer, the National Park Service, that under government policy toward veterans who had been in the Civil Service, my job with National Capital Parks in Washington was being held for me until a given date, with promotions and merit pay raises as if I had been there all along. I had about a month in which to give notification of whether I wished to resume it, and another couple of weeks in which to report for duty if I chose to do so. I had given the matter no thought at all and actually was unaware that the job was being held. Now it looked dazzlingly inviting. I immediately notified the authorities of my intention to reclaim it.

The thought of returning to Washington energized me. I loved the city when I was there before the war; throughout the conflict I retained visions of its beauties and delights. I quickly rounded up my affairs at home, boarded a train, and reported to the National Capital Parks administrative headquarters. I was pleased to find that my boss there was a man I had worked with before leaving Washington and one with whom I was quite compatible. He spent a day reorienting me, driving me around to the major historic sites where I would be working and explaining the new procedures that were in place. He assigned me the plush office in the newly finished Jefferson Memorial, where, except for Jefferson's towering statue, I was the very first occupant.

An amusing development came to light during our reorientation tour. As we approached the Washington Monument, I asked my boss whether a little piece I had written about it back in 1941 had been printed as intended. He pondered a moment, then said no; that it had been recorded orally and was being played over the loudspeaker in the elevator as it ascended to the observation level near the top of the monument. Then he broke into a smile and said that this had produced a remarkable effect on many of the visitors. "Do you recall," he asked, "that we used to have something of a problem there; that quite frequently a woman would faint when she stepped out of the elevator; and that this was invariably accompanied by a loss of bladder control, with most embarrassing results?"

"I do indeed," I replied. And I did recall those episodes. We had kept a bottle of ammonia in the first-aid kit there to be used in reviving the victims.

"Well," he said, "that recording of your manuscript solved the problem. Since we put it in the elevator, not a person has fainted." Years later, a dear friend and colleague of mine, Professor Holman Hamilton of the University of Kentucky, commented upon hearing this story, "Roland, is it possible that this is the most continent prose you have ever written?" Could be!

Washington was still exciting to me. I revisited the Capitol and the many other places that had fascinated me when I lived there before the war. There was now a new structure, the National Art Gallery, which had been completed in 1942 and which captivated me with its beauty. I yet consider it to be one of the most beautiful edifices in the world.

I moved into a large apartment with a number of fellow Tennesseans and prepared to take up life where it had stopped five years earlier. It didn't work: "You can't go home again." Washington had changed and I had changed even more. We staged parties in the apartment and had fun, but I soon became restive again.

An unusual and exciting event did occur shortly after I returned to Washington. I was on duty one day in the Lincoln Museum (Ford's Theater), when I noticed that everyone in the building had gathered into a dense circle near the entrance. Fearing that someone had fainted or that some sort of accident had occurred, I pressed my way through the group, and what I then saw left me somewhat breathless. Standing in the center, with a male escort, was the great and beautiful actress

Ingrid Bergman. I had always immensely admired her in the movies, and had seen her in person when she performed with a USO group in Nuremberg after the war in Europe ended.

I now approached her with uncharacteristic shyness, introduced myself, and offered to show her and her friend through the museum and explain the circumstances of the tragic event of Lincoln's assassination. She graciously accepted, and for about thirty minutes I had the privilege of leading her around the premises with the entire group in tow while I gave my talk. I did this in a semitrance; it was the closest contact I had ever experienced with such a famous and ravishing celebrity.

Despite an occasional incident of interest, the Park Service job now seemed sterile and dull to me, and I soon began to think about returning to school. I worked out what seemed a smart way to do so. By enrolling as a full-time graduate student in George Washington University, I could draw the full tuition and subsistence benefits of the GI Bill; by reducing my Park Service work to half time (twenty hours a week) on half pay, I could carry a full load of graduate work. The Park Service authorities agreed to allow me to do this, and I did so in the last six-week session of the summer, 1947, choosing my old love, history, as a major.

The return to school was fulfilling; I studied seriously and made good grades. Enrolled again for the fall semester, I repeated this procedure. But I now began to become aware that my life was not as rosy as I had anticipated it would be. My work week involved service eight hours a day on Saturdays and Sundays and four hours on Wednesday evenings. This left only the other evenings for studying; I found myself compelled to work until midnight or after almost every night in order to do my schoolwork well. My social life was virtually extinguished; I was caught in a grind.

The manner in which I escaped the grind is a continuing source of wonderment to me and all my acquaintances. At home for the Christmas holidays, I walked into the City Drug Store for a beverage and found my lifelong friend Earl Braden standing at the soda fountain, quaffing a cherry Coke. I had not seen him since we parted for military service five years before. Both of us were overjoyed at the reunion.

After a few minutes of warm greetings, we began to trade our war stories. I, of course, had been a soldier in Europe, he a fighter pilot on antisubmarine duty in the Atlantic. Next we got to the present: I was in school at George Washington University; he was in school at Louisiana State University (LSU). I expressed astonishment when he told me where he was studying; he had been in the University of Tennessee when we got into the war, and our estimation of LSU had been pretty low; we had looked upon it as being the toy of the flamboyant Louisiana politician Huey P. Long. My friend explained that after flying a certain number of missions he was sent back to help train new pilots and was stationed at Harding Field, Baton Rouge. There he met a young woman who was a student at LSU; her presence attracted him to Baton Rouge after he left the service.

When I told him what I was doing, he asked a question that turned out to be the crucial one: "Are you having lots of fun?" I confessed I was not, whereupon he said: "Why don't you come down to LSU? I'm sure they must have a history department there." Upon that casual recommendation, "they must have a history department there," I returned to Washington, finished the semester, resigned my job, boarded a plane, and flew to Baton Rouge. My life was about to take a sea change of unimaginable proportions.

Before I arrived, in January, 1947, Earl arranged to get me a room in the boardinghouse where he lived. He also arranged to get me a job as a waiter in the off-campus restaurant where he worked the dinner shift to supplement his GI subsistence money. I didn't relish such a job but had agreed to take it temporarily; by an immense stroke of good fortune I was saved from having to do so.

When I walked into the LSU history department my first morning in Baton Rouge I was shown into the office of the chairman. A tall, handsome man only a few years older than I sat banging away on an old upright typewriter when I entered. I would have taken him for a graduate student, perhaps a Ph.D. candidate. He swivelled his chair around, thrust out his hand with a smile, and said, "I'm Bell Wiley, department chairman." This little episode began one of the great relationships of my life.

I had never heard of Professor Wiley, but it turned out that he was one of the foremost living historians of the Civil War. His book *The Life of Johnny Reb* was a pioneer work on the affairs of the common soldiers of the Confederacy; his book *Southern Negroes, 1861–1865* was a pioneer work on the life of the slaves during the war and the experience of emancipation.

We chatted a few minutes and learned that both of us were from West Tennessee, our hometowns only about fifty miles apart. He was well acquainted with professors I had studied under at Vanderbilt and George Washington. He liked my Vanderbilt record, which I showed him in the form of a miniature photostatic transcript that I carried in my wallet. That night he telephoned my major professor at George Washington, Wood Gray, and got a favorable report on my work there. The next morning he assured me that I was accepted into the LSU graduate program and offered me a job as his graduate research assistant for the book he was then working on, *The Life of Billy Yank*. I accepted eagerly. I wrote my master's thesis under his direction; it was a study of life on the sugar plantations of south Louisiana during the Civil War.

The immediate effect of getting the job with Professor Wiley was to save me from the waiter's job at the restaurant. The long-range and infinitely more important effect, which I did not fully appreciate at the time, was to provide me the irreplaceable experience of working closely with a scholar of his stature.

To my good fortune, the school that my friend had said "must have a history department" actually had a collection of some of the nation's most brilliant scholars and teachers. This was largely the result of the work of Huey P. Long, who had lavished money on the institution. Political leaders who followed him kept the tradition alive, at least to a degree. This enabled the school to attract outstanding faculty members from throughout the country.

In addition to my work with Professor Wiley, I served for a term as a teaching assistant for T. Harry Williams, who was the most popular teacher on the faculty and whose biography of Huey P. Long, published in 1969, would receive both the Pulitzer Prize and the National Book Award. After Professor Wiley left LSU to go to Emory University, I studied under his replacement, Francis Butler Simkins, whose writings on the history of the American South were among the most distinguished works in the field.

I expanded my master's thesis into a doctoral dissertation under Professor Simkins's direction. He was a brilliant scholar and stylist, but the most eccentric human I have ever known. He did not immediately read the dissertation, but a day or two after each chapter was turned in to him he would say to me, "Charlie, let's go out and read your work under the oaks." We would then go out and sit on a bench under one of the great campus live oaks, where I would read it to him aloud. He would sit with his eyes closed as if sound asleep (I suspect that at times he was asleep), but occasionally he would pop them open and exclaim, "Charlie, that's a magnificent sentence! What the hell does it mean?" I would explain the meaning as best I could, and he would say, "Well then, why don't you just say it that way?" Which is what I did.

Professor Simkins keenly enjoyed his associations with his graduate students. They, in turn, keenly enjoyed him. His quaintly shrewd comments on life were fascinating. He said we veterans had married wives who were more beautiful than Hollywood starlets, and that by working and earning supplementary salaries, they helped provide us with incomes better than that of the chairman of the history department. When we expressed anxiety over the outcome of the formidable oral examinations to which we were subjected, he scoffed: "Ha! They won't fail you fellows. You've swigged whiskey in the bistros of Singapore and beer in the rathskellers of Nuremberg."

Any of Professor Simkins's students could write a book on his eccentricities. Here is my favorite story. He and his wife, Margaret, were married at rather mature ages. Both had been married before, without children. When one day a few months after their marriage he came in from school, she said to him, "Francis, I have something to tell you. I went to see Dr. Smith today." "Oh my," he replied, then asked, "How is Dr. Smith's health?" She replied, "It appeared to me to be excellent. But I didn't go to see him in order to check on his health. Francis, he tells me I am going to have a baby." When Professor Simkins recovered from his shock, he said in great agitation, "Margaret, I feel partially responsible for this."

I studied medieval history under Charles E. Smith, who in my judgment was the most accomplished lecturer on the faculty. I studied also under Government professor Eric Voegelin, a German refugee from Hitler and one of the world's top living intellectuals. I served for two years as a graduate teaching assistant in the freshman course in Western Civilization. This was a great experience for me; I doubtless learned far more in the course than the students did.

I profited immensely from my association with certain of my fellow graduate students. Four of them who were particularly close to me at the time deserve special mention: Otis Singletary, whose work on the employment of black militia during Reconstruction was to win a prestigious award and who would write the volume on the Mexican War published in the *Chicago History of American Civilization* series, and who would become one of the nation's top university administrators, including for eighteen years the presidency of the University of Kentucky; Joe Gray Taylor, who would one day write a history of slavery in Louisiana (a book said by Kenneth Stampp to be the very best state study on the subject), another outstanding book on Reconstruction in Louisiana, and a splendid general history of Louisiana; and Raleigh Suarez, who would become a distinguished administrator in the university system of Louisiana.

The other history graduate student who was destined to play a significant role in my career was Grady McWhiney. He remained at LSU for the master's degree only, and we did not become close friends until years later. He received his Ph.D. from Columbia University, where David Herbert Donald supervised his work. Later McWhiney wrote a number of books on southern and Civil War history, including an award-winning volume on the role of Gen. Braxton Bragg in Confederate defeat.

I received my M.A. degree in 1948 and my Ph.D. in 1951. During the first semester and half of the second semester of the academic year 1950–1951, I served as an instructor on a temporary appointment in the LSU history department. Again, I learned much from this experience. All in all, I believe I received a superior education there; I owe the school an immense debt of gratitude.

As greatly as my life was changed by these academic affairs, it was changed even more by private affairs. My friend Braden was now engaged to be married to the young woman who had drawn him to LSU. Her name was Norma Wright. She was bright and pretty, and possessed an extraordinarily warm personality. She was working as a clinical dietitian at the Veterans Administration hospital outside the town of Pineville, Louisiana, across the Red River from Alexandria, roughly a hundred miles northwest of Baton Rouge.

He hitchhiked his way to be with her every weekend. Soon after I arrived in Baton Rouge he began to urge me to accompany him; he said he needed companionship out on the highway. At first I was reluctant to do so. "What's in it for me?" I would ask him. Eventually, he began to tempt me by saying Norma had made friends with a "very sharp" young woman who was a fellow worker of hers, and that she would "fix me up" with this young woman. That sounded good to me, and in mid-September 1947 he assured me the "fix" had been arranged. The following Friday afternoon we stood beside the Airline Highway, another of Huey Long's gifts to the state, and "thumbed" a ride to Pineville.

We entered the lobby of the nurses' and dietitians' quarters at the VA hospital and Earl announced our presence. Norma emerged at once, and a few minutes later, hearing footsteps in the corridor, we stood and turned, and the most beautiful and most lovable woman I had ever seen walked into my life. I knew in an instant that I wanted her to be mine. Norma made introductions of elegant simplicity: "Allie Lee, Chick." My heart flipped.

She was Allie Lee Aycock, an honors graduate of Northwestern State College at Natchitoches, Louisiana. When I learned where and when she had been in college, I thought how ironic it was that she had been right there only a ten-minute walk away from me when my friends and I were partying in the Hotel Nakatosh during the war. When I said what a pity that we couldn't have met then, she replied tartly, "Oh no, I wouldn't have given you the time of day." Then she explained her dean of women's precautions on the occasions when the "wild men from the woods" came roaring into town.

I pressed my suit to the utmost of my power. Every weekend for the next five I eagerly accompanied Earl on his mission of amour. Indeed, I became the prompter instead of the promptee. The program was strenuous. We hitchhiked up on Friday afternoon, courted ardently throughout much of the weekend, and rode the train back to Baton Rouge on Monday morning, leaving Pineville at 2:00 A.M. and arriving at our destination after daybreak. The train was an antique, probably brought out of retirement and rehabilitated during the war. It bore the name "The Flying Crow"; one of Allie Lee and Norma's fellow dietitians called it the "Creeping Buzzard," a most suitable cognomen. Fortunately, I had no class on Monday mornings. But Earl had an early one, and he had to wait tables at the restaurant that evening. He sleepwalked the entire day.

On my sixth date with Allie Lee, I suddenly asked her to marry me. I flattered myself that the proposal came as a surprise, though I am aware that women are not always as surprised by such overtures as they affect to be. I held my breath for her response.

I must confess, however, that I had already received some intimations of favor. First, the simple fact that she had allowed me to occupy every weekend of her time since our first meeting was a good omen, for in the beginning she had suitors swarming around her like bees around flowering honeysuckle. I had picked up a small signal also in the manner in which she introduced me to her friends and relatives. At first it was Chick Roland, as I had been introduced to her; after two or three weeks she changed that to Charles Roland. Finally, I learned through Norma and Earl that she had stopped dating others during the week while I was absent. The path was clear for me to make an affirmative move.

When I made the move she put me off with one objection or another. I spent most of the weekend attempting to persuade her to accept my proposal. She refused; but when I left her that Monday morning she informed me that we had been invited to have dinner the next Sunday with her sister and brother-in-law in Alexandria—Joy and Keith Weisinger—and that the entire Aycock family was scheduled to be there. I determined to make the best impression possible, just in case.

I dined with the family the next weekend, and I must have made an acceptable impression on them, because before I left for Baton Rouge she informed me that she and Norma were thinking about a double wedding to occur in the spring. I was delirious with joy. As Earl and I rode the train back to school, he told me that he and Norma were planning for her to visit his family in Henderson during the upcoming Christmas holidays; he suggested that I might be able to persuade Allie Lee to accompany Norma and meet and visit my family. I jumped at the idea, and Allie Lee agreed to it.

I wrote my parents of all these plans and they eagerly consented for her to make the visit. I felt confident they would do so, because my mother quite obviously believed it was time for me to be married. Until

I turned twenty-five she had feared that I was about to marry every girl I went out with; afterward, she urgently wanted me to marry every girl I went out with. My parents were exceedingly happy over my prospects of marriage.

Earl and I returned to Henderson at the beginning of the holidays; Norma and Allie Lee came a few days later, just after Christmas. They rode a sleeper on the train from Alexandria to Memphis, and Earl and I met them there; the four of us drove back from Memphis to Henderson. I vividly recall the meeting in the Memphis railway terminal; at first we were unable to see them because they were blanked out by a towering stack of their hat boxes. We did succeed in finding them, however.

My family loved Allie Lee from the moment they met her. As she accompanied my sister Josephine upstairs to her room, my mother turned to me and exclaimed in a rapt whisper, "Son, she is absolutely beautiful." My friends in Henderson quickly fell in love with her also. Numerous of them staged parties for the two of us engaged couples. It was an enchanted occasion.

Near the end of the visit the four of us drove to Memphis for dinner and dancing at the Peabody. I had become impatient with the plans for a spring wedding, and I importuned Allie Lee to agree to be married sooner. That day in Memphis she agreed; we set the date for January 23, 1948; Norma and Earl agreed to serve as the maid of honor and the best man.

I promptly purchased a wedding ring, but when I showed it to my prospective bride she tactfully but firmly said it would never do. She was right. It was undoubtedly the ugliest ring ever manufactured; it was square instead of beveled around the perimeter. I had simply paid no attention to the design. I wisely took her with me when I returned it, and she indicated her preference for simple but elegant rings for the two of us. We have cherished them ever since.

Every wedding day is, of course, unforgettable to the persons married that day. Our wedding day presented a most unusual additional reason for being unforgettable. I was awakened early that morning by a banging on the door of my hotel room in Alexandria. It was my friend Earl, who, as soon as I opened the door, asked me, "Have you looked out the window?" I hadn't, and when I did I was astounded to see snow falling heavily and the ground already covered in a thick blanket of white. It would eventually reach about eight inches, beyond the imagination of anyone alive in the area.

Earl had just come by taxi from the motel where he and I customarily roomed when we were on our courting trips. It was located near the Veterans Administration hospital where Allie Lee and Norma lived. He told me that traffic was badly snarled in the streets and that the bridge across the river was slippery; he advised me to get a taxi and bring Allie Lee back across the stream at once.

I telephoned her immediately, awakening her with the sound of the bell. When I told her about the snow and my concern for getting her across the river, she laughed heartily. "It will all be gone by noon," she said. "Besides, you are not supposed to see the bride until we meet to be married." But she finally gave way to my urgent pleas and consented to come with me. I was able to secure a taxi and made my way to her quarters.

The trip back across the river to her sister's place in Alexandria was an ordeal. By now the streets were extremely slushy and slick, and in places I had to get out and push the taxi with all my might to keep it moving. The first of these was in the driveway of the dietitians' and nurses' quarters. I still have a graphic memory of struggling amid the slush that splashed me from the taxi's spinning wheels. Allie Lee thought the whole episode hilarious. Visible in the corner of my eye, written by our friends in block letters in the fresh snow beside the driveway, were the send-off words: Jan. 23 Allie & Chick.

We were married in the Methodist church chapel in Alexandria. Chaplain Nelson of the Veterans Administration hospital officiated. We had customarily attended his services while we were courting, and we liked his low-keyed style.

I was amazed at my bride's cool calm and ease of bearing; she seemed to have everything under complete control. She says someone in the group had to keep a presence of mind; that I was so nervous I could hardly get the ring on her finger. Earl and Norma stood with us. The two of Allie Lee's sisters who lived in Alexandria, Joy Weisinger and Maxine Southerland, and their husbands and a cousin and her husband were present, as were Allie Lee's fellow workers from the hospital. The snow had so paralyzed transportation in the area that her parents, who lived only twenty miles away, did not make it.

We had planned a honeymoon in New Orleans. The snow prevented it from happening there. Instead, we honeymooned in the Bentley Hotel in Alexandria, where, through an impressive feat of influence with the manager, Keith Weisinger arranged at the last minute to get us a room. We more or less hibernated there for a week because the snow froze and remained that long. I mused at times on the irony of my situation: only a few years earlier, en route to the Louisiana maneuver area, I had spent a night in the Bentley, which at the time was overrun with soldiers in uniform. My memories of the place were decidedly not fond; I had hoped never to see it again. Now it had become a nuptial shrine to me.

For a few weeks after our marriage Allie Lee continued in her job at the hospital and I commuted to Alexandria on weekends. But we soon changed our minds about this arrangement. It obviously was extremely inconvenient for me. I told Allie Lee that I would never get my master's thesis completed if it continued. There was also another factor. Among the dietitians' patients were veterans ill with tuberculosis, and one of Allie Lee's friends suddenly showed positive on the periodic tuberculin skin test. We both felt it urgent for Allie Lee to leave that job and move to Baton Rouge. She did.

Living space was extremely limited. At first we rented a room without any kitchen facilities; we ate all of our meals in the Piccadilly Cafeteria downtown. Allie Lee took a job selling Charles of the Ritz cosmetics at the city's leading department store. After a few weeks we moved into a small apartment. But it was far from both the campus and her place of work. Consequently, we soon moved again, this time to an incredibly small and dingy apartment that had been fashioned out of the attic of a flower shop just across the street from the LSU campus. It was next door to a smelly hamburger joint. Cockroaches abounded.

Finally, we got a veterans' apartment on the campus. These apartments were far short of luxurious; they were converted World War II navy barracks. But they were comparatively inexpensive and reasonably comfortable, and we lived there for the next two years. Allie Lee took a job on campus, managing an eating club for unmarried veterans who lived in dormitories converted from military barracks.

The food was served cafeteria style. It was prepared in the main kitchen on campus and transported to the eating club, where it was reheated and served. This arrangement led to a very pleasant side effect for us. Every Saturday just prior to the evening meal, the club received ice cream in large insulated containers. Because the quantity sent was based on the total number of veterans who held meal tickets, and because many of them were invariably absent from that meal, there was always a considerable surplus even after all who desired seconds or thirds were satisfied. The boarding club's refrigerator had no freezing capacity; the surplus ice cream would not keep, and it could not be returned to the main kitchen because the kitchen closed at the same time the club closed.

Allie Lee solved the problem by giving the surplus to our friends the Singletarys, whose large refrigerator contained a large freezer. The five of us, including Otis, his wife Gloria, and their four-year-old daughter Bonnie, feasted on ice cream before bedtime many nights of the week.

Our first child, a boy, was born on October 22, 1949, while we still lived in our campus quarters. We named him John Clifford, the second part as a namesake of my father. On the occasion of his birth I drove Allie Lee to the hospital in the Singletarys' car, and Otis in effect gave him the diminutive name Cliff, which he would always wear. Needless to say, Cliff was a source of unlimited pleasure to us; we hauled him in a basket to every event we wished to attend. Almost without being aware of it, I had metamorphosed into a dutiful husband and father.

The outbreak of the Korean War in 1949 placed me in a potentially dangerous situation. I had joined the army reserves at the time of my separation from active military service. The inducement to do so was strong at the moment; I was assured that I would never be called back into uniform except during a general national mobilization, in which case I would return to duty as an officer instead of being drafted as a private. This turned out to be a false assurance. As the need increased for troops to fight in Korea, reserves began to be called. I held two of the most sought-after MOS numbers (military occupational specialty numbers) in the army: rifle company commander and infantry battalion operations officer. In the spring of 1951 I received orders to report for an army physical examination.

At about the same date, my former mentor and cherished friend, Professor Wiley, telephoned me that he had recommended me for a position as the assistant to the chief historian of the army, Dr. Kent R. Greenfield. The two of them had worked together in the army's historical division during the war and had become close personal friends. Wiley explained that under the prospective arrangement I would be recalled to active military duty and serve in uniform.

To make a long story short, I was offered the position, accepted it with alacrity, and was recalled to active military duty as a captain and assigned to the Office of the Chief of Military History in Washington. This arrangement probably prevented my being sent to Korea as a combat infantry officer. I felt that I had already "paid my dues" in such a role; my altered status as a husband and father strengthened this point of view. The assignment to serve as assistant to the chief historian may have saved my life.

It also provided me an opportunity to mature significantly as a historian. The major project of the army's historical division was the production of a massive, multivolume history of the United States Army in World War II, one of the most ambitious works ever undertaken in public history. Dr. Greenfield was the architect and guiding spirit of the project. He was a brilliant historian and editor who before the war had been chairman of the Johns Hopkins University history department. I worked for almost a year and a half as his administrative and editorial assistant; in explaining the position to me he said I would be his "man Friday." The experience was the equivalent of holding a high-level postgraduate fellowship for that length of time. I am convinced that it significantly influenced my entire subsequent career.

I profited also from my association with the historians who were engaged in the research and writing of the volumes in the army's series. Two of these figures were of particular interest and importance to me. Charles B. MacDonald had served as a captain and commander of a rifle company in the 2nd Infantry Division. We had shared the horrific experience of being the immediate target of the great German counteroffensive in the Ardennes campaign. He was the author of a splendid little book titled *Company Commander*. He would eventually write two of the volumes in the army's World War II series.

My closest friend in the office was Dr. Forrest C. Pogue, a portly and dignified man who had taught history at Murray State College in western Kentucky before the war. Dr. Greenfield affectionately called him "the bishop." Some of the youths from my hometown had been in Pogue's classes at Murray State. He was at work in the historical office on his path-breaking history of the supreme Allied headquarters in Europe during the war. He had been a combat historian in the war, and we soon learned that he had interviewed me in a dugout on the Elsenborn Ridge a few days after the initial German attack in the Ardennes. Years later, no longer in the Army's historical division, he would produce the definitive biography of Gen. George C. Marshall. I immensely enjoyed his company and learned much from him; we became warm lifelong friends.

Our life in Washington was both exceedingly pleasant and highly educational. I, of course, was back in a city that I had always loved, and Allie Lee soon fell in love with it too. We took every opportunity to visit the city's many places of historical and cultural interest, as well as those nearby, such as George Washington's home at Mount Vernon and Thomas Jefferson's at Monticello. We reveled in the frequent concerts given by the Army, Navy, and Marine Corps bands on the Capitol grounds or the premises of the Lincoln or Jefferson Memorials.

Living in Washington also gave us an opportunity to visit and study the many Civil War battlefields that dotted the surrounding area. I now revisited the Manassas battle sites and made my initial trips to Harpers Ferry, Antietam, Fredericksburg, Chancellorsville, and Gettysburg.

As valuable and enjoyable as my work in Washington was, I yearned to return to teaching. My term of military duty was to expire in the fall of 1952, and during the preceding spring I began to make inquiries and submit applications for a position on a college faculty. At the same time, Dr. Greenfield made me a tempting proposal: he offered me the authorship of an unfinished manuscript in the World War II series, the history of the Allied invasion of southern France. While I was turning this offer over in my mind, I received an offer of a position in the history department of Tulane University in New Orleans. My love for teaching drew me irresistibly toward the classroom and my love for the South drew me irresistibly there. I accepted the Tulane offer, and that September Allie Lee, Cliff, and I left Washington for New Orleans.

In the Classroom Again

Teaching at Tulane was an exhilarating experience for me. I felt that I was now in position to attempt to fulfill the benediction which had been laid upon me during World War II by the Texan who had been a pupil of my grandfather's and had said he hoped I would be as great a teacher as my grandfather.

But in my early years at Tulane I felt inadequate in the classroom, obliged to read compulsively in order to enrich my lectures and discussions with the students. Vanity as well as a sense of dedication spurred me in this effort. I was frustrated also by the realization that I was expected to pursue scholarship, to engage in research and publication—in the parlance of the campus, I must "publish or perish." How to manage both! For some time I felt that I was at the point of perishing. I worked six days a week and well into the nights; frequently, I worked Sunday afternoons and evenings also.

My department chairman, William R. Hogan, did everything in his power to help me. He read my doctoral dissertation, encouraged me to revise it for publication, and played an influential role in procuring me a university research grant for this purpose. I did the necessary revision, and eventually the work was published by a Netherlands press, E. J. Brill, under the title *Louisiana Sugar Plantations during the American Civil War*. The book recounts the vicissitudes wrought by the war on the population of a uniquely colorful section of the Confederacy.

I was somewhat embarrassed over the necessity of paying a subsidy for this service, but my chagrin was erased when the little book received the Louisiana Literary Award of the state library association, with a citation that read: "For the best book published on Louisiana during 1957." The publisher sweetened the occasion of the receipt of the award with an Old World gesture of congratulations by presenting me a dozen long-stemmed red roses. To my delight, the Louisiana State University Press reissued the book forty years later with the slightly revised title *Louisiana Sugar Plantations during the Civil War* and with a new introduction by John David Smith.

Professor Hogan also set me on the path to the major scholarly accomplishment of my career at Tulane, the production of a biography of Confederate general Albert Sidney Johnston. When Hogan learned that I had grown up near Shiloh battlefield and held a lifelong interest in General Johnston, he rather coyly informed me that the largest known collection of Johnston's papers, several thousand items, was located in the university library just across the street from my office. I plunged into the Johnston papers that afternoon.

I remained at this endeavor for eleven years and was greatly assisted by the receipt of a Guggenheim Foundation fellowship that freed me for a full year from teaching, and the receipt of a Tulane University John T. Monroe fellowship that supported my research for two summers. I traveled all over the country, tracking Johnston's movements and searching for documents on his career. In my application for the Monroe grant, I told of visiting the Shiloh battlefield in my boyhood and picking up musket Minié bullets (called "minnie balls" by the soldiers) on the field. After I told this story my colleagues gave me the nickname "Minnie Balls"; even the dean of my college unbent to the point that he once hailed me by this sobriquet.

In 1964 the biography was published by the University of Texas Press under the title *Albert Sidney Johnston: Soldier of Three Republics.* Despite my admiration for Johnston, I freely pointed out the mistakes of his Civil War career, which was cut short by his death in the battle of Shiloh in April 1862; but I concluded that he had already demonstrated the courage, moral strength, will, and decisiveness that are the imperatives of great generalship, and that his death was an incalculable loss to the Confederacy.

My erstwhile mentor Professor Simkins, reviewing the biography for a Virginia newspaper, said that as a former soldier who had observed the realities of war I was able to write about them without voicing "extraneous apostrophes" of disapproval and remorse. He said also that I was able to lay a wreath of laurel on the grave of my hero and at the same time support it with all the paraphernalia of modern scholarship. To my immense gratification, almost forty years after the initial publication, the book was reissued by the University Press of Kentucky with a strong new introduction by Gary W. Gallagher.

While I was at work on Johnston I also wrote another book, a much smaller one than the biography. This, like so many other aspects of my life, came about in a rather unexpected fashion. At the Southern Historical Association convention in Houston in 1958, my Tulane colleague Hugh F. Rankin, a distinguished colonial historian, was being interviewed at breakfast by Daniel Boorstin of the University of Chicago as a candidate for preparing a volume on the colonial wars for the prestigious *Chicago History of American Civilization* series being published by the University of Chicago Press. At the close of their conference Boorstin commented that he needed someone to write a history of the Confederacy for his series. Rankin pointed to me, eating breakfast at the counter, and said, "There's your man."

Boorstin had him call me to their table, and by the time we parted I had agreed to submit a prospectus to him. I did so, and both he and Roger Shugg, the director of the University of Chicago Press, liked it. The result was my book *The Confederacy*, published in 1960.

Perhaps the most exciting professional experience of my Tulane career occurred the following year: my participation in the Northwestern University conference celebrating the Civil War Centennial. The key figure in bringing me into this event was Grady McWhiney, my former colleague in graduate school, now on the Northwestern faculty. He was in charge of setting up the program, and he had already enlisted three outstanding Civil War scholars to deliver addresses: Bruce Catton, David Herbert Donald, and T. Harry Williams. Catton was to speak on the generalship of U. S. Grant; Donald and Williams were to discourse on their divergent views of Lincoln's presidency. McWhiney asked me to speak on the generalship of Lee. Appearing on a program with scholars of such prominence, all of whom either had been or would be recipients of the Pulitzer Prize, was a daunting proposition, but I eagerly accepted the offer.

Allie Lee accompanied me to the conference. I went ahead of her and spent a few days in research at the Illinois State Historical Society on an aspect of the career of Albert Sidney Johnston. She rode from New Orleans to Chicago on the storied Panama Limited train, aboard which she joined Professor Williams and his gracious wife, Stell, for drinks and dinner before retiring to a sleeper for the night. All of us immensely enjoyed the sumptuous festivities surrounding the occasion of the conference.

The four addresses were published by the Northwestern University Press in 1964 in a book titled *Grant, Lee, Lincoln, and the Radicals*. A paperback edition was later brought out by Harper and Row, and it was reissued by the Louisiana State University Press in 2001 with a gratifying new preface by McWhiney and an equally gratifying new introduction by Joseph T. Glatthaar.

Over the years Allie Lee and I became thoroughly addicted to New Orleans. We took moderately to the city's swinging lifestyle and immensely enjoyed its great restaurants, its Dixieland music, its abandonment to Mardi Gras. There is a saying that no other religious zeal equals that of a convert; the same is true of a convert to New Orleans, and we became converts of the most intense ardor.

Our social life in the city at large was equaled by our social life within the Tulane faculty and staff, and especially within the history department. Chairman Hogan and his colorful wife, Jane, entertained lavishly and often in their spacious home on State Street near the campus. The whole department held frequent dinners at such favorite restaurants as Commander's Palace and Delmonico's. Other department members who, with their wives (Betty and Neva), were particularly close to Allie Lee and me were Hugh F. Rankin and Bennett H. Wall. They were outsized men in both physique and personality. I immortalized Rankin by identifying him as "Big Daddy" Rankin; he immortalized Wall by identifying him as "Wall to Wall" Wall. To a degree, the entire experience in New Orleans was one great party.

Both our personal life and my professional life continued at a dizzying pace throughout this period. Our daughter, Karen Jean, was born on December 30 (Allie Lee's birthday), 1955. She began walking and talking at a remarkably early age and added an astonishing measure of zest to our household. Our last child, a boy, was born August 2, 1961.

Allie Lee named him Charles Franklin, the Charles as a namesake of me, the Franklin as that of her father. He was a husky and jolly child who brought us much joy. Our three children gave us a full measure of happiness.

Our entire family enjoyed three great summer trips away from New Orleans during my period at Tulane. The first of these, in the summer of 1962, was a three-week arts and sciences seminar sponsored at Colorado College by the Danforth Foundation. In the summer of 1966 I taught for six weeks at the University of British Columbia in Vancouver, compliments of Grady McWhiney, who was then in the history department there. The next summer I taught at Pepperdine College in Los Angeles. We went by automobile to all of these engagements and visited the places of great scenic and historic interest on the way.

Meanwhile, my teaching and scholarly accomplishments elevated me steadily up the academic ladder; I became an associate professor in 1957, a full professor in 1961. Two years later I was appointed head of the Arts and Sciences Department of History; four years after that to the position of chairman of the university Department of History, which included the Department of History of Sophie Newcomb College (the women's college) and the graduate history division.

In these administrative positions I worked earnestly to improve the teaching and scholarship of the department. Perhaps my most constructive step along this line occurred while I was head of the Arts and Sciences History Department: the creation of a freshman honors program in which incoming students, including Newcomb students, who showed exceptional ability in their high school records and entrance examinations were invited to participate.

The honors classes were small, twelve to a section, and were taught by senior professors, including me. No formal lectures occurred; instead, the students did assigned reading and made oral reports on it, followed by general class discussion. Each student also chose a topic, carried out research in primary sources, and prepared a term paper of at least five thousand words.

The creation of the honors program was in part in response to student complaints that they did not wish to be lectured to, but preferred to learn to think. Some of the students in the honors courses said in their course critiques that their work in this program was demanding

but rewarding; some of them told me later that it was the most rewarding experience of their entire college careers. But to my frustration, a
number of the students wrote in their course critiques that they wanted
to hear more from the professor and less from the other students. In
other words, they wanted lectures. Fickle youth!

I held strong hopes of making a comparable contribution to the
graduate program in history, and the work of my own graduate students continued to be extremely satisfying to me. But outside events
now impinged powerfully on my plans for the department as a whole.
My chairmanship coincided with the most turbulent era in the history
of higher education in the United States, that of the campus protests
against the nation's role in the Vietnam War. As a former soldier who
had risked my life for the nation and had seen many young Americans
sacrifice their lives, I looked with contempt on the pampered students of
the 1960s who protested and demonstrated against the war. Also, as
someone reared under the adage "Cleanliness is next to godliness," I
looked with extreme distaste on the unkempt appearance and obvious
filthiness of the hippies.

I accepted our government's position that we were fighting the war
in an effort to curb the menace of Communism. In later years I have
come to doubt that the menace was as great as it was then represented
to be; I have come to believe also that our effort was doomed to fail
because the American people were not convinced that the national security was as stake. But these altered beliefs have not diminished my admiration for our soldiers who fought courageously, many thousands of
them at the cost of their lives, nor have my altered beliefs erased my
contempt for those who hid their cowardice under the cover of morality and cast slurs on the veterans when they returned home.

The younger faculty, encouraged by a few of the senior members,
took advantage of the student unrest to issue a demand that all faculty
processes be democratized, which in practice meant that all important
decisions, particularly salary decisions, would be made by an elected
faculty executive committee. For a number of reasons, I opposed this
move within the history department. To begin with, it would have vio-
lated existing university policy. Besides, any such arrangement would
have reduced the chairman's authority to a shadow and made him sim-

ply a servant performing the tedious chores for putting into effect the decisions of the committee. I expressed these views to the university provost and the dean of the college and told them I would be willing to step quietly out of the chairmanship if they wished the department to be run in that manner. They assured me that they intended for me to exercise the prerogatives of the chairmanship, that they would hold me responsible for the operations of the department, and that they would accept only my recommendations on all substantive matters involving the department, including that on salaries.

Armed with these assurances, I proceeded to exercise the functions of the chairman as outlined in the university senate document on procedures. The results were not always pleasant, though most of the senior and more-distinguished members of the department supported me; and the business of the department went on steadily though often noisily.

The friction sometimes reached a flash point. After an altercation with a senior professor who was flagrantly derelict in the discharge of his responsibilities, once missing the oral examination of one of his Ph.D. candidates while the professor went fishing, I received from the president of the university a copy of a letter to him in which the professor referred to me as a "lying son-of-a-bitch." When I confronted him with the letter, he groped around for a long time in lighting his pipe, took a couple of puffs, then grunted, "No personal offense intended, Charlie." Eventually, I reassigned all of his graduate students to other professors and began planning steps for his dismissal, a formidable undertaking in dealing with a tenured professor, but he foiled me by suddenly straightening up and improving his conduct markedly. Ultimately, a few of the history faculty, including another senior professor, left Tulane, at least in part because of what they considered the dictatorial way I was running the department.

My relationships with some of the graduate students were exceedingly strained. The most serious of the episodes of tension occurred when I discharged one of the graduate teaching assistants for abandoning his classes for several days in order to participate in a series of off-campus student demonstrations of protest against the Vietnam involvement. I was warned by the campus security officer that the history building would be torched if this graduate student were removed from the classroom. My reply was that he would be removed even if it meant that the building would be reduced to ashes. He was removed and the building was not burned. I also relieved one graduate student of his fellowship for failure to make satisfactory progress on his master's thesis. He argued that the thesis was an obsolete and useless exercise that ought to be dropped, but a majority of the full professors of the department as well as the dean of the Graduate School supported me, and my decision stood.

I had hoped to carry out the duties of the chairmanship without a serious decrease in the quality of my teaching or in the productivity of my research. This proved to be a vain hope. I blocked out an amount of time each day for reading and research, but I found that I could not banish the administrative problems from my mind during these periods. I sat at the desk in my library study, but nothing came forth. I felt increasingly frustrated over the situation; I was being torn away from what I most enjoyed and believed I was best at, teaching and scholarship.

At this time I received tempting offers of positions at two other universities, the University of Missouri and the University of Georgia. The offer from Georgia was especially alluring; it was that of a University Research Professorship in which I would be expected to teach a single course of my preference each semester, with the remainder of my time devoted to research and writing. Reluctantly, I rejected both of these offers.

But in the middle of the academic year 1969–1970 I received an offer of the position of Alumni Professor at the University of Kentucky. It seemed to present a golden opportunity to escape the travails of administration and return to my true profession. I struggled in reaching a decision; the thought of leaving both Tulane and New Orleans saddened Allie Lee and me deeply. But the incentives to do so were very strong. The University of Kentucky was an excellent school, located in a historic and beautiful part of the country, and its history department was particularly distinguished in my field, southern history. In addition, the president of the university was Otis Singletary, who with his wife, Gloria, were our dearest friends from my graduate school days. After an extended period of mental turmoil, I accepted the offer.

We moved to Lexington in the late summer 1970. It would be impossible to exaggerate our homesickness for New Orleans, and I missed the intimacy of the smaller Tulane faculty and the relatively simple administrative processes of that institution. But the decision to make the move proved to be eminently wise. I spent another eighteen years on the Kentucky faculty, came to love the Kentucky undergraduates (most of them), and worked with another group of splendid graduate students.

The most rewarding personal experience of our life in Kentucky was the renewing of our warm friendship with the Singletarys. In addition to the many constructive professional relationships between President Singletary and me, his family and mine have enjoyed countless social occasions together. One of the most gratifying of these is a dinner given by Kendall Singletary Barrett, the Singletarys' youngest child, every Christmas Eve, an affair that has become something of a Barrett-Singletary-Roland institution.

I also renewed a friendship with Carl Cone, a distinguished scholar in English history, who had been on the Louisiana State University faculty during my first semester there as a graduate student. He was chairman of the history department at Kentucky when I came there, and he remained on the faculty for several more years.

I also formed powerful bonds of comradeship with a number of faculty members both inside and outside of my department. The most memorable of these Kentucky colleagues was Holman Hamilton of the Department of History. A former newspaper editorialist from Fort Wayne, Indiana, and a remarkable raconteur, he was an outstanding teacher and a distinguished scholar. We became warm friends and his support of me ensured my acceptance by the Kentucky faculty in general despite a quite natural tendency among some of them to regard my appointment as an example of rampant cronyism by President Singletary.

The most extraordinary academic figure in Kentucky is Thomas D. Clark. I first met him when he delivered the Walter Lynwood Fleming Lectures at Louisiana State University in the spring of 1947, my first semester there. He joined the faculty of the University of Kentucky in 1931 and served as chairman of the Department of History from 1942 to 1965. In 1968 he accepted the position of Distinguished Service Professor at Indiana University. He has published more than thirty books and has served as president of the Southern Historical Association and the Mississippi Valley Historical Association (now the Organization of American Historians).

After retiring from Indiana University, he and his wife Elizabeth Turner Clark returned to Lexington, where we became close friends. A few years after Elizabeth's death in 1995, he married the former Loretta Gilliam Brock. He was then ninety-three. He is now (in 2003) one hundred. He is still vigorously engaged in research, writing, lecturing, and many other activities that support the intellectual uplift of Kentucky and the nation. The state legislature has designated him as the Commonwealth historian laureate for life and as a state treasure. He is more than a scholar of unusual distinction; he is a phenomenon.

In addition to the keen pleasure of my friendship with my history department colleague Professor Hamilton, it paid me great dividends in another way. When I came to Kentucky he was the president of the Kentucky Civil War Round Table, the nation's largest group of this remarkable organization. He immediately brought me into it. My membership and participation in its affairs, including my presidency of it for a number of years in the 1980s, has been a source of immense happiness to me.

My association with the Civil War Round Table led indirectly to a number of extremely rewarding additional chapters in my career. One of our Round Table speakers in the mid-1970s was John Pancake of the University of Alabama. In a casual conversation while he was in Lexington, I mentioned my earlier work in the army's Office of the Chief of Military History. He then told me of a military history conference to be held a few months later at the University of Alabama, the conference theme to be that of the common soldier in American wars. He was to give an address on Yankee Doodle. Among other scholars speaking on the soldiers of other wars were my former mentor Bell I. Wiley, speaking on Johnny Reb and Billy Yank of the Civil War, and D. Clayton James of Mississippi State University, a distinguished biographer of Gen. Douglas MacArthur, speaking on the doughboy of World War I. Pancake asked me to speak on GI Joe, the American common soldier of World War II.

I at once demurred, saying that I would be completely outclassed in such company; that Bell Wiley, for example, knew more about Civil War soldiers than any one of those soldiers knew, and that all I knew about soldiers in World War II was what I had experienced and observed. Pancake said that was exactly what he wanted, and I agreed to be a participant. I sat down to my typewriter and in a few days struck off a paper of about twenty double-spaced pages, entirely from memory. This modest paper would exert a powerful effect on my subsequent career. Throughout the years since my initial presentation of it at the University of Alabama, I have been asked to give it dozens of times at the army's various military schools, including the Army War College, the United States Military Academy, and the Command and General Staff College, on many university and college campuses, and at a conference on World War II held under the auspices of the Roosevelt Institute at Middelburg, The Netherlands.

D. Clayton James had also been a speaker at the Civil War Round Table in Lexington, and I had attempted to persuade the University of Kentucky Department of History to add him to its faculty. Characteristically, they had vetoed the proposal. I say "characteristically" because many of the younger members of the department who had come into it in recent years frequently vetoed my proposals as being those of an old fogey. James was now serving a year as the Harold Keith Johnson Professor of Military History at the Army Military History Institute and the Army War College at Carlisle Barracks, Pennsylvania. He returned there from the Alabama conference and strongly recommended that I be brought as his successor. In the spring of 1980 they invited me to come, and I accepted.

My year at Carlisle Barracks (1981–1982) was a remarkably interesting, invigorating, and pleasant period. My primary duty during the fall semester was to conduct a seminar on worldwide strategic issues, and during the spring semester a course on the American Civil War. The students at the War College were selected from the very best of the officers of field grade in the army and Marine Corps; they constituted the group from which the future generals would be chosen. There were also a number of officers of similar grade from "friendly" other nations. All of the students were extraordinarily bright and conscientious. As in my previous teaching experience, I unquestionably learned more from them than they learned from me.

My year at Carlisle Barracks overlapped with my presidency of the

Southern Historical Association (1981). This honor had come to me as the result of my overall academic accomplishments. But it was the immediate reward for the production of two books: *A History of the South* (published in 1972), coauthor with Francis Butler Simkins, and *The Improbable Era: The South since World War II* (1975). The first of these volumes was originally written by my former mentor Professor Simkins and was the textbook on southern history I had studied as a graduate student at Louisiana State University. It was, in my opinion, the most comprehensive, most insightful, and most brilliantly written single-volume history ever produced on the region. Following the author's death in 1966, the publisher, Alfred Knopf, upon the suggestion of Mrs. Simkins, asked me to revise and update the book with credit as the coauthor. I was flattered and pleased at this invitation and readily accepted.

The second of the volumes that gained me the presidency of the Southern Historical Association was in a very real sense a byproduct of the first. An editor from Random House, which had absorbed the college publications department of Alfred Knopf, asked me to expand my chapters on the recent South into a separate small book, which I promptly did. But the manuscript became a victim of editorial reshuffling at Random House, and the book eventually was published by the University Press of Kentucky. The central theme of this work holds that though the post–World War II South experienced the most striking changes of any region of the country, it nevertheless remained the most distinctive of all the regions.

The presidential address I delivered to the Southern Historical Association was titled "The Ever-Vanishing South." It embodied the theme of the book *The Improbable Era* with additional discourses and illustrations supporting it.

My work as the visiting professor of military history at Carlisle Barracks led to another assignment with the army that I found richly rewarding and exciting. I spent the academic year 1985–1986 as the Visiting Professor of Military History at the United States Military Academy at West Point, New York. During the fall semester I taught three sections of twelve to fifteen student cadets each in the general military history course; that spring I taught two sections of a course in the Civil War. The Civil War course was easy for me; it was in my primary field of research and I had given the course before. But the general military history course kept me at my desk until late every night studying to stay one step ahead of the cadets, an effort that was not always successful.

My students this time were undergraduates. They were eager and energetic and, not unexpectedly, better disciplined than the usual run of students in a civilian university. The cadets were, on average, also abler students. This was the result of the Military Academy's higher entrance threshold (which, if applied at a civilian state university, would have eliminated perhaps the bottom 20 to 30 percent of the students) and of the discipline that assured virtually perfect daily class attendance.

The experience at West Point was immensely stimulating. I was impressed by the dedication and diligence of the faculty and staff, and everyone was hospitable and kind to Allie Lee and me. We entered fully into the West Point spirit, which follows the motto: "Work hard, play hard." My time at West Point, as I have indicated of my time at Carlisle Barracks, provided a tremendous education for me.

Overlapping with this year at West Point, I enjoyed the honor of serving as the chairman of the Department of the Army Historical Advisory Committee from 1985 until 1987. This group is composed of members from the various army schools and historical offices plus a number of distinguished military historians from universities throughout the country.

I returned to Kentucky and taught there for two more years before retiring at age seventy at the end of the spring semester 1988. In spring 1991 I experienced one of the most exciting events of my career, comparable to the occasion of the Civil War symposium at Northwestern University thirty years earlier. I delivered in Eisenhower Hall at West Point, to the entire military history course (over a thousand cadets), a lecture on General Eisenhower as an operational commander. For this lecture, I drew upon my own experience as one of General Eisenhower's soldiers as well as upon my editorial work in the Office of the Chief of Military History and my considerable independent reading on World War II in Europe.

During the last ten or twelve years of my teaching in Kentucky I devoted a significant amount of my time and energy to the general editorship of a series of books on the American South titled *New Perspectives on the South,* published by the University Press of Kentucky. The director of the press suggested the idea of doing the series and asked me to be the general editor. I became the architect of the series, chose the subjects, recruited the authors, approved the prospectuses, and read and accepted or rejected the manuscripts when they were submitted. I adopted a format quite similar to that of the *Chicago History of American Civilization* series in which my book *The Confederacy* had appeared. Each volume in my series represents a compressed synthesis of 50,000 to 100,000 words on a selected subject in southern history.

Thirteen volumes have appeared in the series. All have received favorable professional reviews, some have received extraordinarily favorable reviews, and two have received national awards: Gilbert C. Fite, *Cotton Fields No More: Southern Agriculture, 1865–1980*, the Theodore Saloutos Memorial Award of the American Agricultural History Association for the best work on the subject published in 1984; and Albert E. Cowdrey, *This Land, This South: An Environmental History*, the Herbert Feis Award of the American Historical Association, for the best book by a nonacademic historian published in 1983. I am proud of the series.

During my teaching career I, of course, served on countless university committees, much of the work of which was exceedingly boring. Most of the committees seemed to me to be engaged in mere "busy work." But some of them played important roles in academic affairs. I enjoyed my service on the Tulane University Research Council, a group that decided which research proposals were to be funded; this work seemed to me to be of outstanding importance.

But the committee assignments that were most gratifying to me were connected with the University Press of Kentucky. I served for sixteen years as a member of the university press committee and of the editorial board of the University Press of Kentucky, a publishing consortium that includes all of the state universities, a number of the leading private colleges and universities of the state, and the historical societies of the state. For almost half of this time I occupied the chairmanship of the committee and the editorial board. I believe the Press is one of the most creative and distinguished departments of the entire state university system.

As affairs turned out, my teaching career was not quite over when I retired. Shortly before the Eisenhower lecture, I received an invitation to return to West Point for a year as the Visiting Professor of Military

History. Forbidding as was the prospect of making another move, Allie Lee and I had so enjoyed our previous time there that we agreed to go back and did so for the academic year 1991–1992. Having formerly taught the courses, I found them easier for me to handle this time.

Teaching the Civil War both in the general history course and in my special elective course was easier for another reason: I could use my own book as a textbook. At the suggestion of a Random House editor in the mid-1980s, I had begun work on a brief, comprehensive history of the Civil War. This book was published in paperback in 1991 by McGraw-Hill, which had absorbed the Random House College Department, and in cloth cover by the University Press of Kentucky. The title is *An American Iliad: The Story of the Civil War.* The West Point history department had already adopted it as the text for the relevant portion of the general military history course, and when I returned to West Point I adopted the book for my elective course.

Again I enjoyed working with the cadets, and they seemed to enjoy my teaching. They appeared to appreciate particularly my ability to draw upon my own war experiences for analogies to the events they were reading about. Some of their comments in their course evaluations were memorable. For example, that of a young woman cadet, "His lectures are just like storytime"; or that of a young man majoring in engineering, "Too much like a history class." The department chairman was so amused by the latter remark that he posted it on the departmental bulletin board.

My teaching at West Point on the second occasion led to another exciting experience: a lecture trip to Europe. Col. Charles F. Brower IV, deputy head of the history department, was scheduled to spend the academic year 1992–1993 at Middelburg, The Netherlands, as the representative of the Franklin D. and Eleanor Roosevelt Institute. One of Colonel Brower's accomplishments in this capacity was the staging of a great conference on the last year of World War II in Europe. He invited me to deliver a lecture on my own experiences in the war.

The conference occurred in the spring of 1994. Many outstanding military historians from all the involved nations participated, making it a remarkably informative affair. Allie Lee accompanied me, and we immensely enjoyed our time exploring Middelburg. Afterward, we extended the trip to Bruges, Belgium, a gem of surviving medieval architecture set amid so many canals that it is often called the "Venice of the North." From Bruges we traveled to Amsterdam, a city of infinite color and variety. Its most haunting spot, which we visited, is the attic where the Jewish teenager Anne Frank and her family were hidden for two years during the war. Though she eventually was captured and died in a Nazi concentration camp, her diary represents an incredible testimonial to the endurance of the human spirit.

My intention for years had been to use my retirement time for the completion of a research project begun shortly after coming to the University of Kentucky—a biography of former Kentucky governor, United States senator, and national commissioner of baseball Albert Benjamin "Happy" Chandler. I had heard of him before coming to Kentucky, but I knew virtually nothing about him. It was impossible to live in Kentucky without learning about him; he had been one of the most important, and one of the most controversial, political figures in the state's history, and possibly the very most colorful of its citizens. He was still vigorously alive and frequently in the newspapers.

My interest in Chandler was kindled by serving as a fellow member of the university athletics board. He seemed bigger than life; he was surrounded by a veritable personality force field. I decided to write a biography of him, and for something like twenty years I collected information for this purpose. His papers, hundreds of thousands of them, are in the university library; President Singletary generously provided funds for a research assistant to work through the immense collection while I pursued the more urgent task of interviewing Chandler and his associates, including both supporters and critics. I completed a great number of these interviews, including ones with the notorious political figure George Wallace and the renowned football coach Paul "Bear" Bryant.

As matters turned out, however, I had not reckoned with my own declining energy or with other projects that now appeared to claim it. The years spent at the military schools took me away from the Chandler project altogether. Also, I took time out to write *An American Iliad*. Eventually, I got down to the business of writing a draft of the Chandler biography though I was fully aware that additional research would be required to finish it. I completed what I estimated to amount to about

20 percent of the manuscript, the section covering Chandler's birth, early years, and entry into Kentucky politics.

But this came slowly and painfully; I clearly realized that I was suffering a severe case of burn-out. Finally, and reluctantly, I decided to turn the project over to someone else, someone who possessed the energy to finish it. The person chosen, Dr. Thomas H. Appleton Jr., had served for twenty-one years as the editor of the Kentucky Historical Society's journal, the *Register*. He had exhibited a rare degree of professionalism in this capacity. I was convinced that he would bring this quality to the Chandler biography and that it would in turn enhance his career. Appleton accepted the opportunity to complete the biography as a collaborative work in his name and mine.

As events occurred, I was destined, to my surprise, to publish two more books prior to writing this memoir: a brief, interpretive work on Robert E. Lee, titled *Reflections on Lee: A Historian's Assessment*, issued by Stackpole Books in 1995, and *Jefferson Davis's Greatest General: Albert Sidney Johnston*, issued by the McWhiney Foundation Press in 2000.

The provenance of these volumes is rather unusual. A year or two before I came to the University of Kentucky, I was asked to prepare a text on Lee for a book of photographs and excerpts from his papers to appear in an extensive biographical series titled *Illustrious Americans* that was being published by the Silver Burdett Company, a division of General Learning Corporation. I wrote and submitted my manuscript and received payment for it, but the series was canceled without the book being published. I filed away a carbon copy of the work and more or less put it out of mind.

In the 1970s and 1980s a number of books harshly critical of Lee appeared in print. They accused him of being so enamored of Virginia or so myopic that he was unable to see the Civil War as a whole; or that he was so wedded to Napoleonic military concepts that he was unable to adjust his strategic and tactical thinking to the age in which he fought: that he employed eighteenth-century tactics against nineteenth-century technology. I considered these criticisms to be tendentious and unbalanced, using speculative arguments to sustain their points of view.

As I discussed these writings and their perceived flaws with my friends in the history profession, they urged me to write my own views on Lee.

Finally, I divulged the existence of my manuscript, and William C. Davis, consulting history editor of Stackpole Books, invited me to submit it to that company. I did so, and after I had completed a number of corrections and revisions, Stackpole brought it out. It does not whitewash Lee's mistakes. Yet it concludes that he accomplished as much as, if not more than, anyone else could have done with the limited resources at his command; that he was a great general and a great human being, and that these two qualities were mutually reinforcing.

Meanwhile, my longtime friend and benefactor, Grady McWhiney, who had retired from the position of Lyndon Baines Johnson Professor of American History at Texas Christian University and had sponsored a press in his name, asked me to submit an abbreviated version of my biography of Albert Sidney Johnston for publication by this press. I did so, and the book named above is the result. As with Lee, a number of historians had in recent years severely disparaged Johnston's generalship, accusing him of having been indecisive and negligent. I disagree with their evaluations, and this gave me an opportunity to refute their views to the best of my ability. I repeated my earlier conclusions that Johnston was indeed decisive and possessed of strong moral as well as physical courage, that he displayed an extraordinary capacity to inspire his troops, and that his death deprived the Confederacy of a leader of Lee's stature in the western theater of the war.

I have relished my retirement career, which has been filled with preparing book reviews for the professional journals, evaluating manuscripts for these journals and for a number of university presses, publishing the brief studies on Lee and Johnston, and writing an essay on Confederate general P. G. T. Beauregard that is supposed to be published in a book devoted to the full generals of the Confederacy. In addition to these activities, I have been engaged for several years in lecturing all over the nation, once in Europe, and repeatedly on the great river steamboats the *Delta Queen, Mississippi Queen,* and *American Queen.*

The pleasure of lecturing on these occasions has been greatly heightened by the presence of friends and fellow speakers who represent the most distinguished group of living Civil War historians. Many of my lectures have been delivered before Civil War Round Tables or at conferences held under the auspices of the Deep Delta Civil War Symposium at Southeastern Louisiana University, the Shenandoah University McCormick Civil War Institute in Winchester, Virginia, under the directorship of Brandon Beck, or the Civil War Education Association with headquarters in Winchester, Virginia. The director of the Civil War Education Association, Robert Maher, schedules an especially delightful conference at Sarasota, Florida, every January, which affords an opportunity for all of us from the colder climes to thaw out briefly in the middle of the winter and to discuss our favorite topic while doing so. I could not have dreamed up a more enjoyable form of retirement.

My home life has been rich. My wife, Allie Lee, has been a constant companion and has encouraged and assisted me in all of my undertakings. We have entered enthusiastically into the social and cultural affairs of the University of Kentucky, a situation enhanced by our close ties with the Singletarys. We have also developed many enduring friendships with townspeople who are not connected with the school. We have enjoyed to the utmost the University of Kentucky athletic contests, especially basketball, a sport in which our teams have won three national championships since we came to this state.

There have, of course, been times of sadness. The keenest of these were at the deaths of our parents. My mother died in 1984, a few days short of eighty-eight years of age. My father died a year later at ninety-two. My brother Paul died shortly after the death of my father. But my parents had lived long and happily. They would not have wanted their children to grieve excessively over their passage. I am forever grateful to them for all they did for me.

Throughout my career our lives have been embellished by travel and by our residence in such cities as Washington, New Orleans, Vancouver, Los Angeles, and West Point as well as in Lexington. My speaking engagements and various academic conferences have taken me all over the country, and Allie Lee has accompanied me to the more exciting places. We have tremendously enjoyed occasional trips to Europe, where I have revisited the sites of my wartime experiences and have visited many of the most historic and enchanting cities of England and the Continent. We feel that we have lived full lives.

In Retrospect

In looking back over my life, I believe I could not have chosen a more satisfying profession than that of teaching and scholarship. These activities have precisely suited my taste and personality. I was extremely fortunate in being the offspring of parents and grandparents who imbued me with a strong thirst for knowledge and the means of acquiring a sound formal education. I was equally fortunate in being able to study under mentors who imparted to me the most precious gift a teacher can bestow: the capability to teach myself. Finally, I have been blessed with a patient and loving wife who has encouraged and supported me unstintingly; without her, I could not have done anything comparable to what I have done.

Though I have never entertained any desire to repeat my military service, I am convinced that it added a significant dimension to my career, especially to that portion dealing with martial history. It taught me self-discipline and perseverance, qualities that are vital to any field of endeavor. It also gave me an insight into the nature of my fellow human beings, and particularly into that of war and soldiers, an understanding that cannot be gained from books. I learned at the existential level the true meaning of Clausewitz's famous dictum concerning the ubiquity of "friction" in war: a meaning captured perfectly in the World War II soldiers' pungent acronym SNAFU ("Situation normal, all fucked up").

My odyssey through the expanses of history has convinced me that it is a vital sustaining force in society. It records, of course, the full range of human motives and actions, ignoble as well as noble, and thus can lead its votaries into cynicism and despondency. But I support the view expressed by Robert E. Lee near the end of his life when he wrote that his experience of men had not disposed him to think worse of them or indisposed him to serve them, nor had the many errors and failures which he had come to recognize caused him to despair of the future. He said the march of Providence is so slow, the life of humanity so long, and that of the individual so brief that we often see only the ebb of the advancing wave and are thus discouraged. "It is history," he concluded, "that teaches us to hope."

I have not been an especially prolific scholar, but I take pride in the books and articles which I have produced. They are unique to my character and experience; nobody else could have written them as they are written. I take pride also in the students I have produced, particularly the eighteen graduate students who prepared their doctoral dissertations under my direction, nine at Tulane University and an equal number at the University of Kentucky. They represent a variety of points of view, some of which differ from my own. This does not upset me; I had no desire to clone myself in my students. Instead, I sought to encourage them to think for themselves and demanded only that they diligently pursue the sources and support their conclusions with convincing evidence, logical reasoning, and clear and concise expression.

Some of my students have surpassed me, or will do so, in the volume or excellence of their work. This pleases me because I look upon their careers as an extension of my own. I have read or heard it said that Socrates' greatest contribution was the production of his student Plato, and Plato's greatest contribution the production of his student Aristotle. What a bracing thought on which to end these memoirs!

Appendix 1

Charles P. Roland's Ph.D. Students and
Their Present Professional Status

GRADUATES OF TULANE UNIVERSITY

Albert E. Cowdrey: chief, Conventional War Studies Branch (retired), United States Army Center of Military History; adjunct professor of history, University of New Orleans; consultant, National D-Day Museum

Clara Lopez Campbell D'Aquilla: instructor (retired), Mississippi Gulf Coast Community College

John L. Ferguson: Arkansas state historian and head, State Archives

Roger A. Fischer: professor of history (retired), University of Minnesota Duluth

William Gabard: emeritus professor of history and director of International Studies (retired), Valdosta State University

Donald E. Reynolds: emeritus professor of history and head, Department of History (retired), Texas A&M University, Commerce

Bobby W. Saucier: emeritus professor of history, Dillard University

Leon C. Soulé: associate professor of history (retired and deceased), Cleveland State University

V. Jacque Voegeli: emeritus professor of history and dean, College of Arts and Science (retired), Vanderbilt University

GRADUATES OF THE UNIVERSITY OF KENTUCKY

Thomas H. Appleton: professor, Eastern Kentucky University

Dwayne Cox: head, Special Collections and Archives, Auburn University

Melba Porter Hay: division manager for Research and Publications, Kentucky Historical Society

Jerry B. Hopkins: assistant professor of history, East Texas Baptist University

Carol Reardon: associate professor of history and scholar in residence of the Civil War Era Center, Pennsylvania State University; adjunct faculty, United States Marine Corps Command and Staff College

Jason Silverman: professor of history, Winthrop University

John David Smith: Graduate Alumni Distinguished Professor of History, North Carolina State University

Richard Smoot: associate professor of history, Lexington [Kentucky] Community College

Thomas Syvertson: adjunct professor of history, University of Louisville

Appendix 2

Charles P. Roland: Emeritus Alumni Professor
of History, University of Kentucky

PRINCIPAL PUBLICATIONS

Louisiana Sugar Plantations during the American Civil War. Leiden: E. J. Brill, 1957. New edition titled *Louisiana Sugar Plantations during the Civil War,* with a foreword by John David Smith. Baton Rouge: Louisiana State University Press, 1997.

The Confederacy. Chicago: University of Chicago Press, 1960.

Albert Sidney Johnston: Soldier of Three Republics. Austin: University of Texas Press, 1964. New and revised edition, with a new Introduction by Gary W. Gallagher. Lexington: University Press of Kentucky, 2001.

"The Generalship of Robert E. Lee," in *Grant, Lee, Lincoln and the Radicals,* ed. Grady McWhiney. Evanston: Northwestern University Press, 1964. New edition, with a new Preface by Grady McWhiney and a new Introduction by Joseph T. Glatthaar. Baton Rouge: Louisiana State University Press, 2001.

A History of the South. Coauthor with Francis Butler Simkins. New York: Alfred A. Knopf, 1972.

The Improbable Era: The South since World War II. Lexington: University Press of Kentucky, 1975.

An American Iliad: The Story of the Civil War. New York: McGraw-Hill, and Lexington: University Press of Kentucky, both 1991. Revised edition, New York: McGraw-Hill, 2002.

Reflections on Lee: A Historian's Assessment. Mechanicsburg, Pa.:Stackpole Books, 1995.

Jefferson Davis's Greatest General: Albert Sidney Johnston. Abilene, Tex.:
McWhiney Foundation Press, 2000.

New Perspectives on the South series. General editor. 13 vols. Lexington: University Press of Kentucky, 1979–.

SCHOLARLY AWARDS AND HONORS

Louisiana Literary Award, 1957; John Simon Guggenheim Foundation Fellowship, 1960–1961; president, Louisiana Historical Association, 1969–1970; University of Kentucky Award for Excellence in Research, 1977; Center for the Study of Southern History and Culture, University of Alabama, Victor Hugo Friedman Distinguished Visiting Professor of Southern History, 1977; president, Southern Historical Association, 1981; University of Kentucky Department of History Hallam Award as outstanding professor, 1979–1981; University of Kentucky Research Professorship, 1980–1981; Department of the Army Outstanding Civilian Service Medal and Citation, 1982; chairman, Department of the Army Historical Advisory Committee, 1985–1987; United States Military Academy Commander's Medal for Outstanding Service, 1986; Kentucky Civil War Round Table Townsend-Hamilton Award for distinguished accomplishments in Civil War history, 1989; Secretary of the Army's Decoration for Distinguished Civilian Service, 1992; Phi Beta Kappa membership in recognition of high attainments in liberal scholarship, 1994; Chicago Civil War Round Table Nevins-Freeman Award for outstanding contributions to American history during the period of the Civil War, 2000; Civil War Education Association William Woods Hassler Award for "exceptionally meritorious contributions" to the field of Civil War studies, 2001